Afrika |

AT WAR

Below: Looking tired and dishevelled Generalfeldmarschall Rommel is pictured here in his staff car during the withdrawal.
/R. James Bender/The National Archives

Afrika Korps
AT WAR

2.The Long Road Back

George Forty

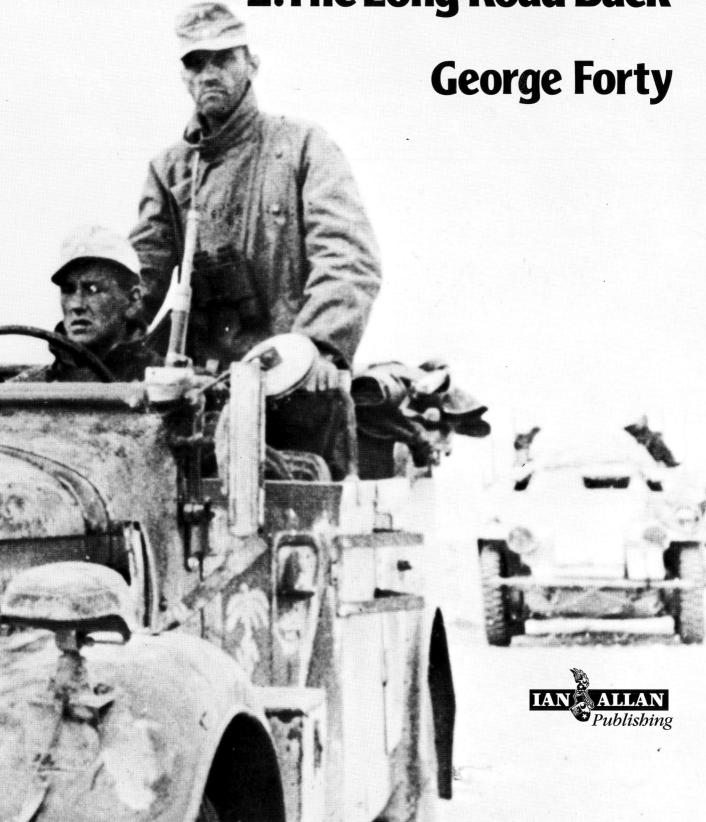

IAN ALLAN Publishing

First published 1978
This impression 1998

ISBN — Ian Allan Publishing edition   0 7110 2580 0
ISBN — Vanwell Publishing edition   1 55068 092 7

Published by Ian Allan Publishing

an imprint of Ian Allan Publishing Ltd, Terminal House,
Station Approach, Shepperton, Surrey TW17 8AS.
Printed by Ian Allan Printing Ltd, Riverdene Business
Park, Molesey Road, Hersham, Surrey KT12 4RG,
England.

Code: 9809/A2

Below: Part of Rommel's rear guard coming out of
action with their captured British 25 pounder. As soon
as all the kit is loaded they will withdraw to a new gun
position./*Bundesarchiv, Koblenz*

Contents

Panzer rollen in Afrika vor

Worte von einem unbekannten Soldaten
Musik von Norbert Schultze

Ueber die Schelde, die Maas und den Rhein
stießen die Panzer nach Frankreich hinein.
Husaren des Führers im schwarzen Gewand,
so haben sie Frankreich im Sturm überrannt.
    Es rasseln die Ketten . . . es dröhnt der Motor . . .
    Panzer rollen in Afrika vor!
    Panzer rollen in Afrika vor!

Heiß über Afrikas Boden die Sonne glüht.
Unsere Panzermotoren singen ihr Lied!
Deutsche Panzer im Sonnenbrand
stehen zur Schlacht gegen Engeland.
    Es rasseln die Ketten . . .
    Es dröhnt der Motor!
    Panzer rollen in Afrika vor!

Panzer des Führers, ihr Briten, habt acht!
Die sind zu eurer Vernichtung erdacht!
Sie fürchten vor Tod und vor Teufel sich nicht!
An ihnen der britische Hochmut zerbricht!
    Es rasseln die Ketten . . . es dröhnt der Motor . . .
    Panzer rollen in Afrika vor!
    usw.

Introduction

This second volume begins in January 1942, with the Afrika Korps back in Tripolitania, licking their wounds and preparing for another all out drive on Cairo and Alexandria. Rommel had no intention of remaining on the defensive any longer than was absolutely necessary, and, just as soon as he had received sufficient new equipment, fuel and reinforcements, he attacked, with the same dazzling success as he had achieved in 1941. There followed some desperate days for the British, weakened by the long arduous campaign of the previous year and once more at the end of a tortuous supply line. The elastic had again been stretched too far and they were rapidly forced to give ground. As we shall see Rommel was even more successful and almost won the most glittering prize of all, the Suez Canal, which would have undoubtedly changed the whole course of the war. But it was not to be. With dogged stubbornness the British line held against the last despairing attacks of the almost exhausted Afrika Korps. The 'throw for Alex' did not succeed and from then on the writing was on the wall for the Germans and their Italian allies, and the eventual defeat of Rommel's forces only a matter of time. It was left to a newcomer to win the greatest of all the desert victories and Monty's name will for ever be linked with his triumph at El Alamein.

So, apart from their exhilarating start, this book should tell a tale of defeat for the men of the Afrika Korps and I suppose it does. However, few armies have ever carried out a more dogged, hard fought and orderly withdrawal over such difficult terrain. Even when the Operation Torch landings had taken them in the rear the Desert Foxes were still able to show their teeth at Kasserine. Their record is one that any army would be justly proud of achieving and their ultimate surrender holds for them no less glory than did Dunkirk for the gallant survivors of the BEF.

I must again thank everyone who has helped me with this book. The many contributors are mentioned, as in the first volume, throughout the text with their reminiscences and photographs. Their generosity and kindness is much appreciated. Again I must thank General der Kavallerie aD Siegfried Westphal for writing the Foreword for the first volume. I felt that, with his unique knowledge of the Afrika Korps and their great leader, no one else could possibly have done the task quite so well. I am also most grateful to Harcourt Brace Jovanovich Inc for permission to quote from the American edition of B. H. Liddell-Hart's *The Rommel Papers* in both this and the first volume.

Some readers may wonder why I chose to quote, as part of the dedication in both books, from a poem, written by an Englishman about his school chapel and a memorial inscription to a British soldier who was probably killed on some outpost of the Empire, well before World War II ever started. It is a poem which I learnt as a boy and one which has always had a profound effect upon me – *Sed miles, sed pro patria* – could any man who loves his native land wish for a better epitaph?

Macht als vorwarts, Jungs!

Bradford, Yorkshire   *George Forty*
January 1978

Far left: Panzers Roll into Africa
(Words by an unknown soldier –
    Music by Norbert Schultze)
Over the Scheldt, the Meuse
            and the Rhine
The tanks thrust on towards
            France
Hussars of the Führer dressed in
            black
Thus they overran France by
            force.
    The tracks clank . . . the
            engines roar
    Panzers roll on into Africa!
    Panzers roll on into Africa!

Hot above the African sands the
            sun burns down
Our tank engines sing their song
German tanks in the sunshine
Stand ready for the fight against
            England
    The tracks clank . . . the
            engines roar
    Panzers roll on into Africa!
    Panzers roll on into Africa!

Tanks of the Führer, you
            Britons beware
They are intended for your
            destruction
They fear neither death nor the
            devil
On them British pride will shatter
    The tracks clank . . . the
            engines roar
    Panzers roll on into Africa!
    Panzers roll on into Africa!
[Brig P. A. L. Vaux

Left: One of the favourite
mementoes of North African
service was a hand-made ring
bearing the Afrika Korps symbol.
They were available in unit
canteens or from local merchants.
[R. James Bender

Rommel Strikes Backs

The Desert Foxes Lick their Wounds

Having been forced to withdraw out of Cyrenaica the Afrika Korps set to work to rebuild its strength. It was remarkable what an effect on morale a few days rest made, particularly because new equipment, fuel and supplies were now available in reasonable quantities. You will remember that we left Wolfgang Everth fighting a confused rear-guard action near Mechili, this next extract from his diary radiates new confidence:

'*19.I.42*

The quiet days are doing us a power of good. One can sleep a bit by day and have time for oneself. Military things also look a bit rosier. There is now enough fuel, and due to the containment of Malta by our flyers, the convoys are again arriving in Tripoli. The tank regiments are getting some new vehicles and new weapons are also arriving, some of them – anti-tank guns and fighting vehicles –

Russian. Since we have once again become somewhat stronger, the English – so I have heard – are to be attacked immediately, if they dare to attack us. Yet they have become somewhat half-hearted and move forward very carefully, beside which they have had tiresome work with our mines. Yesterday the wireless reported the fall of Halfaya Pass. Great commiserations over those magnificent fellows who have fought there. To hold for two months, completely encircled on all sides, in an area of two kilometres by one kilometre, is nothing less than a unique form of heroism and it is not in any way comparable to the fortress of Tobruk. Now the Tommy has freed more of his troops and has an easier supply route. We hope he will attack the Korps – we can now deal with him properly from our positions, but I think he feels he isn't strong enough. In the evening a CO's Conference. The orders: the unit will move north during the night. Will we attack? It

Below: Preparing to advance. The tank commander of a Pz Kpfw III carefully scans the horizon shortly before advancing. The half track crew behind him also appear keen to discover what lies ahead.
|Associated Press

Left: Tank tracks in the sand. The panzers of the Afrika Korps move forward once again across the sands of Cyrenaica, reaching almost to the very gates of Cairo and Alexandria.
/Bundesarchiv, Koblenz

Below: Moving through the desert wastes, units of the DAK strike back into Western Cyrenaica.
/Bundesarchiv, Koblenz

Bottom: MG Battalion 8 on the march to Msus during the reoccupation of Western Cyrenaica by the DAK. The rear vehicle is towing one of the new 5cm anti-tank guns, which was designed by Rheinmetall-Borsig and entered service in late 1940 under the designation 5cm Pak 38.L/60./*H. D. Aberger*

seems likely. Troop leaders briefed for the night march. Then snatch a quick sleep. It is incredible how quickly the days have already got longer – at Christmas it was dark by 1745 hours and only slowly got light again at 0730 – now it isn't dark until 1845 and is light again at 0645.

20.1.42
Reveille 0330. Moved off to the north at 0600 in darkest night. I went on ahead. In Maaten Giofer at 0700 and waited 3½ hours in a *ghibli,* which blew strongly, on orders from Korps. We went on to the area of Korps HQ, about 25km SE of El Agheila, arriving 1430. CO went to Korps HQ to find out the situation. Slowly the remaining vehicles of the unit came up; they had got stuck fast in the soft sand and had to work hard to free themselves. Two of my recce vehicles fell out with clutch damage. My little force was vanishing again! Capt von Meyer came back from Korps HQ with thick orders. It is indeed true that *we* will attack in the morning. Tommy is said to be weaker than us in his forward areas, and through recent deliveries of equipment Rommel has again got his toys.

'Situation discussed, troop leaders briefed, Günther's and Behlendorf's troops go out early tomorrow to recce. They have a difficult task for many of our mines have been laid whose *exact* position cannot be ascertained even from the best minefield plan, since no firm datum points exist in the desert. It grew late with all the preparations and briefings and everyone quickly crept away, for who knew what efforts lay ahead of us'.

The Attack Begins

On 21 January 1942 Rommel issued a Special Order of the Day to his troops:

'German and Italian soldiers!

You have fought hard battles against an enemy superior in numbers, however, your morale is unbroken.

At the moment we outnumber the enemy immediately in front of us. The Panzergruppe will therefore launch an attack today to defeat them.

I expect every soldier to give of his best during these decisive days. Long live Italy! Long live the great German Reich! Long live the Führer!

The Commander in Chief
ROMMEL
General der Panzertruppe'

Continuing to quote from Wolfgang Everth's diary we get a 'sharp end' view of Rommel's second offensive, which was to prove just as successful as his earlier lightning campaign:

'*21.1.42*

The Column rolls! At 0630 the recce troops march off. We placed ourselves to the east of Korps HQ and waited for the first reports. Our recce and fighter planes were up and Stukas flew eastwards. At long last in the right direction again! The leading division received artillery fire. Recce troops reported English columns moving back. Günther's troop captured three English howitzers with their vehicles and an OP vehicle, and took three prisoners. Prima! On the horizon stood columns of smoke – Tommy had set fire to his unserviceable vehicles. Stukas and fighters continuously roaring overhead. No English aircraft to be seen the whole day. Slowly we moved forward through the thick sandy going. Behlendorf's troop reported to his front a hundred abandoned English vehicles, including 12 howitzers and eight SP anti-tank guns. Tommy must have bolted sharpish. The leading division turned northwards, to close the sack with the Italian tanks coming down from the north. There certainly ought to be something in the sack. Hope so. Next day will tell. As it became dark went into close leaguer with Korps HQ to act as their protection, 25km SSE of Mersa el Brega.

Parties sent out to salvage captured lorries, guns and ammunition – things we urgently needed. A further three of my vehicles sent back with failures and other damage and the next day saw me with seven vehicles, of which six were out by night on patrol so that only one remained with me! Fourteen of my vehicles are back in workshops and can't be repaired because of the bad spare parts situation. If it goes on like this I will soon be bankrupt. It is however said that resupply of spare parts is due at Tripoli.

22.1.42

Reveille 0600. The unit is to recce the best route for the Korps to the Via Balbia. Then Tommy should be encircled from the north. Since there are no more recce troops, I went out myself with the MT sergeant and the Signal NCO. Going terribly sandy. Finally found a route which is to a certain extent usable. The unit, plus Korps HQ, went on to the NNE, far ahead of my three signal trucks. No one knows exactly where he is, so my good minefield plans are of no use. One must rely on one's feel, and one's lucky stars, and so we got on alright. Stukas again at work. On the horizon there was a thick wall of smoke and dust. Again two recce vehicles fell out, the wireless vehicles of all things. Now only one recce troop still up with the enemy, and this with only two vehicles. I called in the remaining vehicles and sent the damaged ones to workshops. The weather is good, nicely warm. A lack of cigarettes for weeks. In despair one smokes the Italian one

pfennig cigarettes. They taste of nothing but produce dense smoke. In the afternoon we reached the Via Balbia near El Brega and from there were to go to Agedebia, which, because of the columns on the march, we only reached at 2000, at dusk. On both sides of the road still lay our own mines from the withdrawal, and a number of shattered English vehicles lay in the minefields. By night the mines were troublesome for us too: in their ignorance some of our own vehicles drove on to them. They weren't laid for this! In Agedabia the unit got orders to go on at once to Msus (135km NE of Agedabia) in the desert. Filled up, then away. Our own forces are already ahead but are to halt and close leaguer after 50km. Now began a frightful night march. Slowly we moved forward through mud and clay on tracks with scarcely any foundation. It was pitch dark. My own vehicle stuck fast and it took two hours before it was freed. We were cold, tired and only kept awake by the foul cigarettes, the "long torpedos".

23.1.42

In the morning we came to Antelat, where a German unit was already leaguered. From here on with our small band we were right in front. Two large English aircraft of an old type, apparently courier planes, flew away quite low over us. One was shot down in flames, and the other had to make an emergency landing. Slowly our unit collected itself together after the night march. We went on again at about 0900, three recce vehicles of

Top left: Air reconnaissance. A Fieseler Storch light recce aircraft swoops low over a tank column as it advances through the desert. This excellent little aeroplane was capable of taking off and landing in extremely short distances, it was also almost impossible to stall and could fly at very low speeds./*K. Susenberger*

Centre left: The Fog of War. An artillery barrage raises clouds of choking dust and smoke during a desert battle. /*Rommel Museum, Herrlingen*

Bottom left: A Pz Kpfw III. Note the 3 Panzer Division symbol on the front of the upper hull. This symbol was carried by AFVs originating from 3 Panzer Division which formed 5 leichte Division. The large figures on the side of the turret denoted the vehicle identification number. These digits indicated: First number – the company number. Second number – the platoon (*Zug*) number. Third number – the AFV's position within its platoon (tanks 1-5). /*Christopher Foss*

Below: Up the pole! A novel Italian artillery observation post, February 1942./*IWM*

mine, two patrols from the motorcycle company and Kiehl had one captured English gun. That was all! The rest were in workshops. An 88mm AA gun and an artillery battery were also with us, in support. After 12km the lead troop received artillery fire from Tommy and reported a position with anti-tank guns, vehicles and infantry. Our artillery took up a fire position and opened up. But we had to be sparing with the ammunition. So it went on for several hours – we couldn't advance, and on the flanks there were English armoured cars. To our left vehicles appeared, first twenty, then a hundred. Everyone looked through his glasses and came to the conclusion they were German. We wanted to join in parallel to them, to force a way ahead. But when they were 4,000m away they turned out not to be Germans. There was also artillery with them, and plenty of it. Tommy turned and disappeared northwards. A bit later behind us, to the right, another large column appeared on the horizon making towards us. At first they were also taken for Germans, but a recce vehicle which had been sent out raced back again and reported that they were English vehicles and artillery. So once again the old situation – enemy all round. There was only one thing to do – a few shots over the bows of the column and then move back quickly as possible, so as not to become cut off. As the enemy column got bigger and bigger, we went back in the direction of Antelat and engaged with everything we had. Lo and behold, Tommy turned and withdrew north. English fighters in the air today as reconnaissance. Evening came and with it a supply vehicle with the mail! A letter from my father dated 10 January already here. Juffa sent a postcard of snow covered mountains. What a contrast! In the evening we went into close leaguer near Antelat and hoped to be able to snatch some sleep. The day had been tiring but night could be even more so. Zicurke's troop brought back four prisoners in the evening, together with a small truck, which had come right up to the muzzles of his guns.

24.1.42

We were in luck! The night passed quietly and without incident. Reveille 0600, CO's Conference 0630. New task: to attack SE in a broad gap between the German Afrika Korps and the Italian Motorised Corps, in conjunction with the latter. 0900 – in position 20km south of Antelat and were then formed up. In front of us Tommy was wheeling about, but his main body must already have been pulled out of this area during the night. The attack went with a lively speed for sixty kilometres. As I had no more armoured cars, for the troop had been taken by Rommel, I travelled in the signal truck to the flank as observer and screen. We found a few abandoned English vehicles and destroyed them. By chance I saw a remarkable little hummock, looking almost like a bush. I moved up to it and saw from a distance of ten metres that it

was a light tank covered with camouflage nets. A man clambered out and seeing my machine pistol raised his hands. Since the tank was a non-runner (though it should have been able to shoot!) we doused it with petrol and let it die a fiery death. That one would be no further trouble to anyone! At our destination we halted and indeed had no more petrol, but new orders were already to hand; immediately back to Antelat (80km) and reconnoitre to the north. But no one could alter the fact that firstly we had no fuel and secondly no recce troops. So we waited in the desert for our fuel tender, which had long since been despatched. We hoped they would soon find us, for it was already 1600. At 2100 when it was completely dark, the convoy arrived. We filled up. New task: to move 40km north to Saunu, thence to advance NE at 0700 the next morning. Moved off at 2200. I led. Here a few words on moves in Africa; if the going allows it, one travels in columns. Recce vehicles travel within sight, ahead and on the flanks, like destroyers at sea. In a group at the front the anti-tank guns and the headquarters group, the artillery in the middle and the echelons and an anti-tank gun at the rear. Speed about 20-25kph depending on the going. By night one normally travels in three columns close together, at about 5-10kph. In darkness, when one can't see, the vehicles have to endure a great deal because one bumps over the boulders and the heaps of stones and sand like a ship in a Force 10 gale. As commander one balances oneself along-

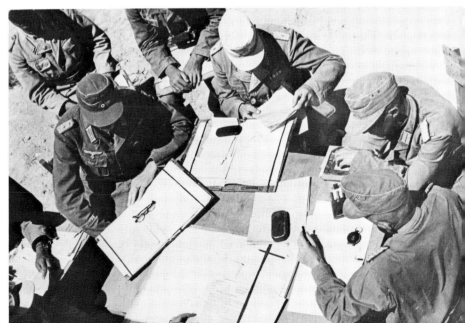

side the driver, constantly watching the needle and the luminous mark of the compass. One is continually saying "a bit more left, further, good, now a bit to the right". This goes on the whole night. Great fun! But sleeping would be nice. Now back to the story. The night march went forward well, my wireless blared music by Zara Leander and Grete Weiser and our captured English cigarettes cheered us.

25.1.42

By 0200 we had gone 40km, but of Saunu – by now surely nothing but a pile of stones – we could find no trace. And that would indeed have been a coincidence. We slept – wonderful! At 0530 came our new orders: move at once to Antelat, advancing from there at 0800 with the Motorcycle Battalion on Msus. Still 30km to go to Antelat: moved off at 0600, still in complete darkness. After 15km my vehicle stopped. I thought it was nothing much and the unit went on. But the petrol pump had broken and only after an hour's work was it put right. In front of us the noise of battle. The unit is already through in Antelat and attacking. Here I heard that the Tommy was still in Saunu during the night and only withdrew early today. And we had slept perhaps within a kilometre of him. Damn! I rejoined the unit and we were soon engaged in an artillery duel. To our right our troops were advancing. Vast numbers of smoke plumes on the horizon Tommy was setting fire to his fuel dumps. Behind us came an English heavy tank which surrender-

Top: The crew of a Panzer III wearing a mixture of headgear (the visored field cap and the black field cap). Note also the Dutch pith helmet hanging outside the tank and the symbol denoting the destruction of a British fighter on the gun barrel. /R. James Bender/The National Archives

Above: After their initial spectacular successes the DAK paused to build up its strength for the all out drive on to Cairo and Alexandria. The photograph shows the rest camp of MG Battalion 8 in the great wadi west of Timini, April 1942. /H. D. Aberger

Right: Action stations! MG Battalion 8 start up their motorcycles to resume the offensive./H. D. Aberger

ed after a shot from our 88. Our supporting artillery was again taken away from us. We decided to rename the unit "An 88mm AA gun supported by trucks and lorries (formerly the AA3)". Together with other troops of the Afrika Korps, Msus was taken. Here there was a large English supply depot, partly burning. I went up to it to look for POL. I found petrol, water, tyres – then I was off after rations. A vehicle from the Motorcycle Battalion raced up signalling, pointing out some English transport which had come up and was already within 30m. So I stepped on the gas and raced back to the unit who had noticed nothing. Tommy had also taken us for his own troops since we almost exclusively travelled in English trucks. In all, from where we were we could see an English convoy of 8 guns, 10 AFVs and 40 lorries. The convoy came towards us to a distance of 1,500m. Now all hell was let loose. The 88 and our captured English gun engaged over open sights. Success! Tommy pushed off, leaving several trucks, a gun and two AFVs behind. The gun was retrieved: now we have two – our strength is increasing! The old position – Tommy all round us. Everywhere the noise of battle and columns of smoke. We are to remain here for the time being. Other units of the Afrika Korps are attacking North-East and North-West. It is already 1700 and one is bone-tired. But in an excellent mood – since the beginning of the offensive on 21 January we have already travelled over 500km (as far as Berlin to Könisberg!). When Tommy had withdrawn I sent out a party who soon came

upon a new English lorry loaded with petrol and they brought back tinned milk, fruit jam and biscuits from the supply depot. My company now consisted of a signal truck, an English ration truck, an English water tankette truck, one armoured car with Rommel and two armoured cars back from workshops. Will we be able to sleep tonight? It is already 1900 and no new orders yet received. 2100 air alarm. Everything brightly illuminated with parachute flares and some bombs fell. Tommy, doesn't seem to understand that one needs a bit of rest.

26.1.42
The night passed quietly. We obtained further things from Tommy's supply dump and slowly made ourselves become Tommies, our vehicles, petrol, rations and clothing were all English. I was somewhat international too: Italian shoes, French trousers, German coat and hat, English linen, stockings, gloves and blankets. A soldier's life is fine! Devoured everything, put on new linen and had some rest. Tommy, this is our revenge for the things you have done to us! Breakfasted off two tins of milk, a tin of pineapple, biscuits and Ceylon tea. Unfortunately the reality of war soon returned again. The English made a low level air attack on our echelon, which had come up to us early. Four men were killed and several wounded, it was reported on the wireless. A truck came up to us, halted and out got two Englishmen. Until midday we loaded up English petrol, filling it into German cans which were better. The English

Below: A Panzer II light tank is dwarfed by a Sd Kfz 251 reconnaissance half track as the crews discuss plans on the Via Balbia, 27 June 1942.
/*Bundesarchiv, Koblenz*

tin cans were too weak – 4,000 litres – splendid work! The captured vehicles were painted with German crosses, so as to achieve at least some difference. At 1300 came the order that we were once again under our Division and were to go there. We set off and found them in the evening about 25km east of Msus. There we placed ourselves in line to defend the Division's front. At 2100, in darkness, came our Echelon, on which the air attack had been made. They now reported that one NCO and six men had been killed and some men very seriously wounded. Men from my company were also there – dreadful. The night was quiet'.

The Afrika Korps offensive continued until late January by which time Benghazi had fallen and the British were back on the Gazala line. It was during this offensive that Sir Winston Churchill made a personal reference to Rommel in a speech to the House of Commons on 27 January 1942. He said: 'I cannot tell what the position at the present moment is on the western front in Cyrenaica. We have a very daring and skilful opponent against us and, may I say across the havoc of war, a great general. He has certainly received reinforcements. Another battle is even now in progress and I make it a rule never to try and prophesy beforehand how battles will turn out'.

Baptism of Fire

For the next few months from February to May there was a lull in the fighting whilst

Above left: Members of a signals battalion in May 1942. Note the knee length tropical boots worn by two of the signallers. The other is carrying a map or despatch case (*Meldekartentasche*.) /*R. James Bender/The National Archives*

Left: A tank column stops for a short halt on the Via Balbia – I wonder if there was Chianti in the bottle? 27 June 1942. /*Bundesarchiv, Koblenz*

Above: Orders Group in progress outside a Sd Kfz 251/6 half track which was the divisional command post of a panzer division (the metal pennant is black, white and red). Taken during the offensive of January – February 1942./*IWM*

Right: Achtung Spitfire – take cover!/*Bundesarchiv, Koblenz*

both sides again built up their strength, Rommel urged the High Command in Berlin to attack Malta and thus secure his lines of communication across the Mediterranean, but his pleas fell on deaf ears. So, when he realised that further delays could only help his opponents, he decided to forestall an enemy offensive and attacked the Gazala line on 26 May. There followed another period of heavy fighting with the British being forced back once again, culminating in the final surrender of Tobruk. For some soldiers, like Karl Susenberger, this attack in late May was a 'baptism of fire'. Here is how he remembers it:

'On the evening of 25 May whilst orders were given out it was made known that the battalion was leaving. The tents were taken down, all equipment stowed away, the lorries were filled up, etcetera. On the morning of the 26 May when the battalion was ready to be off we moved up to the front of the regiment, and waited for the final order to march. We didn't have long to wait. Round about noon the powerful armada of vehicles and tanks started moving; the direction was

Top: French gunners engage the enemy over open sights in their tenacious defence of Bir Hacheim in late May 1942. For 14 days and nights the garrison under General Koenig held out until 11 June when they had to evacuate their positions./*La 13e Demi-brigade de Legion Etrangere*

Above: The DAK pressed home its attacks on the Bir Hacheim position with great determination. Here a 5cm anti-tank gun belonging to the third company of MG Battalion 8 engages British tanks near Bir Hacheim on 2 June 1942./*H. D. Aberger*

Left: An Sd Kfz 233 on patrol. This version of the standard German eight wheeled armoured car mounted a short barreled 7.5cm gun./*IWM*

south, the name Segnali-Sud. For us common soldiers that didn't mean much, what it meant we only found out later. Towards evening the order was given to stop, but at about 2100 we went on again and indeed travelled all that night. When it became light we had an hour's rest. We didn't have to wait long for the first English recce aircraft, we fired at them with our flak and shot one down. After the rest the march carried on uninterrupted until midday when we stopped once more. In front of us a big tank battle was hotting up and the English artillery shells were landing only 200 metres away from us. Our tanks won the battle and moved forward. Meanwhile, we learnt that we had detoured round Bir-Hacheim during the night. We went past some knocked out tanks and stopped once more by a ruin. I saw a Tommy sitting in a hole, his head was laid right back, his helmet had slid from his head to one side, around him was a swarm of flies. I wondered if he was alive and jumped from the vehicle. When I got up to him I realised he was dead. He was buried on the spot, his hidey-hole became his grave. Next we came

into the environs of Acroma on the Trigh Capuzzo and took up position near the track. Near the battalion HQ an 88mm gun was put into position, should Tommy try anything on he would get a proper reception, but the English artillery didn't wait for long and soon put down harassing fire. They swept the whole area with fire. Suddenly a sandstorm blew up and we sheltered in our holes or vehicles. After about a quarter of an hour we heard the sound of vehicles coming nearer, as we put our heads out of our holes we saw a number of English carriers that had lost their way in the sandstorm. After a small amount of shooting the Tommies gave themselves up.

'Next morning the artillery fire started again, it seemed to come from all sides and we felt we were surrounded. The low-flying English aircraft were also there and strafed us. One was shot down and crashed west of the Trigh Capuzzo. More noises of aircraft engines replaced them – a formation of Stuka's flew over and, before we could lay our smoke signs, they turned on their left wings and dived onto our own position.

Below: A despatch rider (with his message between his teeth?!) prepares to leave a command post Sd Kfz 251/6 half track. /IWM

Above: German artillery pound
the defences of Tobruk. The gun
is a 10.5cm leichte Feldhaubitze
18 which had a maximum range
of 10,675 metres, which was
increased later to 12,325 metres
by increasing the muzzle velocity.
A single baffle muzzle brake
(*Mundungbremse*) was then fitted
to accomodate the extra recoil
forces./*IWM*

Right: A Bersaglieri despatch
rider from the Italian Ariete
Division arriving with a message
at an Sd Kfz 263 eight-wheeled
radio car./*IWM*

Far right, top: British colonial
troops taken prisoner near Bir
Hacheim make their way to the
POW cage./*Burdesarchiv, Koblenz*

Far right, centre: German artillery
men pose beside a captured
British Morris C8 4x4 'Quad'
field artillery tractor used for
towing field guns and ammunition
limbers./*W. Susek*

Far right, bottom: Inspecting a
captured British Crusader tank,
taken during the offensive in
January 1942./*H. Long*

When they realised their mistake, they jettisoned their bombs, but a few hit anyway. The 88mm flak and its towing vehicle were hit, a few vehicles burned and we suffered some casualties. In the middle of all this mess the Tommies attacked and could only be thrown back with great effort. The oaths that came from every mouth were not repeatable. Suddenly we saw Major Ehle and Lt Kordel driving in the direction of Division. After a long time we saw Kordel come back alone and we learnt that Major Ehle had been wounded by a low-flying attack. The battalion was taken over immediately by Captain Reissmann. Towards evening we were told to get ready to move out. On the morning of 1 June 1942 the battalion stood ready on Trigh Capuzzo to attack the strongpoint Got el Ualeb.

My First Action

Shortly before the attack began radio operator Grimm and I were detailed by Lt Kordel to act as runners. As it was our first action we were naturally mighty scared and who hasn't felt this way before their first action? Our preparations took place in the basin of Trigh Capuzzo so that the enemy couldn't see us. The attack was scheduled to begin at 0715;

Above: Recently captured British POWs are taken off for interrogation in a Volkswagen Kfz I./*IWM*

Left: Elements of 15 Panzer Division move into battle through the smoke of burning vehicles./*Col T. Bock*

Top right: A Panzer IV Model F, with the short L/24 75mm gun, engaging a target. The side hatch is open so that empty shell cases can be easily jettisoned. /*Brig P. A. L. Vaux*

Centre right: Inspecting one of a group of knocked out British Matildas./*Brig P. A. L. Vaux*

Right: Artillery in action at Bir Hacheim, 27 May 1942, the scene of a heroic defence by Free French Forces, who resisted all attacks during 14 days of savage fighting, as Rommel sought to occupy this vital southern pivot of the Gazala line. /*Bundesarchiv, Koblenz*

perched on the vehicles we waited, I had my machine pistol with three replacement magazines on its sling. I was in low spirits with all sorts of confused thoughts going through my head. I thought hopefully "you'll make it, you won't die at only 19". I looked over at Grimm, he obviously felt the same way. All at once our Stukas came over and their bombs fell right on the English stronghold. Scarcely had they let the last bomb fall then everything started to fire and an immense wall of dust loomed up in front of us, blocking Tommy's vision. We came within 600 metres of the strongpoint before the defensive fire began. Now we got out of our vehicles and moved forward in an extended line, we tried to get nearer the English by moving in bounds. Their defensive fire got fiercer and the first wounded began to call for the medics. It became increasingly difficult to get forward especially as we could see practically nothing of their front line. I remained always close to Lt Kordel so as to be on hand quickly. Crouching, jumping and running in zigzags we reached the first English barbed wire. I had taken cover behind a camel thorn bush and was bathed in sweat, my throat was so dry that I took a hefty swig out of my water bottle. The Sappers were there and, in spite of the murderous defensive fire, they had to clear a path through the minefield so we could go through. The lads were superb, they managed it. Our heavy weapons, artillery, pak and 88 flak carpeted the English positions. About 0900 we succeeded in breaking in.

'From the forward positions we took between 90 and 100 prisoners, but it wasn't

over yet. Lt Kordel called to me "Susenberger come with me, we'll bring the 20 millimetre forward". We both dashed away and succeeded in getting it up to the point at which we had broken in. From behind artillery and the 88 boomed even deeper into the stronghold. By midday we had taken a large portion of the British positions. The prisoners had increased in numbers and Grimm and I received the order to take them to the rear. More and more came out of the depths so we had to make the journey several times. Towards 1600 the stronghold fell and we counted 1,800 prisoners. Eight of us had to take them back to Division which lay about three kilometres behind. This was a hard bit of work because the column kept getting split up, so that we had to watch it very closely. After handing them over at Division

our driver, Bernd Rey took us back to the stronghold. We saw now the havoc wreaked by our heavy weapons; dead lay everywhere, burnt out tanks, lorries, guns etc. On the journey back to the battalion we saw an English tent standing in a small depression. Bernd drove right up to it to see what was happening and with machine pistols at the ready we went up to the tent and fetched 10 Tommies out of it, who were hiding there. We disarmed them, but had to take them back to the battalion on foot because they wouldn't fit in the car. Having arrived back at the battalion we reported back to Lt Kordel and he said "Where on earth did you pick them up?" Bernd reported everything and on Kordel's orders had to take the Tommies immediately back to Division.

Above: A gun crew from 190 Artillerie Regiment prepare to move off. Their gun is the Russian 7.62cm which was issued to the regiment in April 1942 just before the May offensive. It was known as the 7.62cm FK296(r) and saw action on all fronts. The Germans even went as far as producing their own ammunition for this sturdy, reliable field gun. /*W. Susek*

Left: Members of an artillery unit stop during the advance to look over a knocked out British Matilda tank./*W. Susek*

Above: **German infantry attack across the open desert, supported on the right flank by tanks.** */Bundesarchiv, Koblenz*

Right: German infantry occupying British positions which they overran on the perimeter of Tobruk during the May offensive 1942./*Col T. Bock*

Below right: Tobruk falls. The first German vehicles enter the fortress and park in the main square, 21 June 1942./*IWM*

'I came out of my baptism of fire fairly well but slightly bashed, this was endurable. We then set out to march on the Trigh Capuzzo in regimental and divisional formation.'

As I have explained this attack saw the final capture of the fortress of Tobruk, for which Rommel was promoted to Field Marshal – the youngest in the German Army. The announcement of the fall of Tobruk was made from the Führer's headquarters on 21 June 1942:
'The Commander of the Army lets it be known that under the orders of General Oberst Rommel, Italian and German troops stormed most of the strongly defended positions of Tobruk. Today an English flag of truce the position was surrendered to an Italian Corps Commander. The town and harbour were occupied. 25,000 prisoners of war, including many generals, were taken and an unknown quantity of weapons, war materials and provisions. In a tough follow up against the British in the east, Bardia and Bir el Gobi were also taken'.

Charging an English Strongpoint
Werner Susek, a gunner in the 3rd battery of 190 Artillerie Regiment also remembers the 'push' that summer, and wrote the following short account of an action in which he took part:
'During the push in the summer of 1942 we, the 3rd battery of Artillerie Regiment 190 were at times part of Battle Group 288, commanded by Colonel Menton. We were often engaged with the English when we met them in the desert. I remember one morning

when the order to attack was given. After driving for a while we reached the middle of a plain about three kilometres wide. There we got the order to take up positions for firing. The tractor drivers turned and we brought the four Russian long range guns into position. Ahead of us the German infantrymen had been forced to take cover for, in front of them was an English minefield and behind it, on the high ground, English infantry had taken up positions. They had a lot of machine guns and because of their good fields of fire our infantry could not make any progress. Behind us a big German howitzer battery was firing, but it was too far away. As soon as we had brought our guns into position the order came: "Enemy position in front 1,000 metres, fire". All four guns fired. The shells hit their marks exactly. The English were demoralised by this direct shell-fire and soon surrendered. They got out of their trenches and holes with their hands raised, and came safely through the minefield to join us. They were quickly searched, but were allowed to keep their personal things and then waited to be moved to a prison camp. Now our infantry made a pathway through the minefield and, together with our chief, Lieutenant Schreiber, his driver and radio operator, they occupied the hillock. Shortly afterwards we received the order from them: "One gun must be sent forward". The decision fell to the gun on which I had the job as second gunner. We drove through the mine-path. It took our breath away when we saw the barbed wire entangling in the chain of the engine. The driver didn't notice anything and drove like hell. We expected

Below: Tobruk harbour becomes the scene of intense activity as the DAK begin to use it as a supply base./*Associated Press*

that the whole lot would blow up at any moment, but we reached the hillock unhurt. The infantrymen were pressing themselves to the ground and called to us to take cover because of snipers. A pity we were unable to follow this well-meant advice as we had to bring our gun into position which, with its height, gave the enemy a pretty easy target.

'We moved our gun forward until the barrel pointed over the top of the hillock. Lt Schreiber then ordered: "Enemy anti-tank gun in front of us, 50 metres, fire". I will never forget this situation, when we fired our gun at such an enormously short distance. After we had fired a few shots, Lt Schreiber called "Forward march, march!" He and the infantrymen stormed forward, the chief firing with his tommy-gun.

'Meanwhile we inspected the English trenches and looked for booty. The things we found were very suitable for us, especially the food. Some comrades invested themselves with clothes, for the English were well equipped. But we found something that was still more interesting namely, exact drawings of the guns, gun-carriages etc. of our division. Thus they knew exactly what kind of enemy they faced. Suddenly we heard the loud voice of Lt Schreiber: "Why are you still squatting there? The enemy resistance has been broken for a long time". Hardly had he said this when a bullet whistled past. Whether we wanted or not, we couldn't help smiling at the face he made. In the meantime something had happened behind us. One of our trucks had been damaged by a mine and some comrades were wounded. Furthermore, a 3.7cm anti-tank gun, which had been ordered to support us, had been hit and its crew wounded. We got ready to return to our starting point. A medical officer crossed the battlefield to take care of the wounded, waving a white flag. After returning and short rest we were ready for new actions that were certainly waiting for us'.

The guns which Werner Susek mentions were 7.62cm field guns which had been captured on the Russian front and could be used both as anti-tank or field guns. They had a maximum range of about 14 kilometres.

Forty Miles from Alexandria
After a short pause to regroup Rommel continued to advance driving the British back well beyond the frontier to the El Alamein positions. This was the only defensible line between 'the Wire' and the Delta, so the British knew that there could be no withdrawals if they were to remain in North Africa, thus, it was the turn of GHQ Middle East Forces to issue a Special Order of the Day:

Left: Tobruk, after the breakthrough on 20 June 1942. The Companies of 1st Bn Armd Inf Regiment 104 (MG 8) had taken posts R62, R65 and R67 in the first and second defence lines. (L to r: Maj Schuette – Bn Comd; Hauptman Prahl – OC 1 Coy; Lt Schulz – Adjt). In the background is a 2cm Flak 38 mounted on a Demag D7. /H. D. *Aberger*

Below left: Just before the assault on Tobruk began the MG Battalion 8 had become 1st Battalion Armoured Infantry Regiment 104 (MG 8). (L to r: Maj Schuette – Bn Comd, Generalmajor Von Bismark – Comd 21 Pz Div, Oberst Ewert – Comd of Armd Inf Regt 104). /H. D. *Aberger*

Right: The commander of the 1st Battalion Armoured Infantry Regiment 104 (MG 8) confers Iron Crosses on soldiers who earned these awards during the assault on Tobruk, June 1942. /H. D. *Aberger*

Below: After Tobruk has been captured. A South African General and his Adjutant meet Oberst Ewert, the Commander of Armd Inf Regt 104 (in the pith helmet)./H. D. *Aberger*

'*Special Order of the Day*

The German/Italian Forces are trying to force their way into the Delta to capture Cairo and Alexandria and drive us from Egypt.

It is the duty of every officer and soldier to stand firm and fight the enemy wherever he may find him, regardless of the cost.

The results of the whole war may well depend on how we conduct ourselves in this great battle. As brothers in arms we must have confidence in ourselves, in each other, and in our weapons and determination to win or die. This is the fighting spirit which will give us victory.

SOLDIERS! DO YOUR DUTY.

H. R. ALEXANDER
General
Commander-in-Chief
Middle East Forces'

By this time, however, the Afrika Korps was all but exhausted, short of all types of supplies and equipment, in particular battleworthy tanks. Indeed, having started in late May with about 400 tanks, Rommel had now a mere 50 left in action. Nevertheless he continued to press forward and at the end of August attacked the El Alamein line. To close this section here is another extract from Ralph Ringler's diary, in which he describes their abortive attack on the Alam Halfa Ridge. This was a key position and, in order to attack it Rommel had swung the DAK well south of the main British line, then turned north so as to take Alam Halfa from the flank. After two days of bitter fighting he was, however, forced to withdraw.

'2.9.42
My lads lay in makeshift dug-in positions on an overhang. It was very difficult to get the PAK (anti-tank gun) into place, she had to be so deep that only the muzzle showed out. It wasn't quite light when the British bombarded my positions with heavy artillery fire. The sounds of tanks could be heard in the whole area. The Chief (Oberstleutenant Frommel) didn't want to be caught napping so, somewhat prematurely I thought, gave the tank alarm warning. That made the young, inexperienced soldiers panicky and I had to try to calm them down. I ran from foxhole to foxhole and spoke about false alarms and endeavoured to quieten them. In spite of this there reigned a feeling of terrible confusion throughout the company. Who had withstood a tank attack before? None of us. A tank attack almost without protection, almost without any possibility of cover ... Kismet said to us "fight or be overwhelmed", running was no alternative. In the dawn light I saw a "Bandit" (enemy tank) that started to fire at our position with its machine gun and main armament. The Chief had been right after all. I ran to the PAK and gave orders to engage the "Bandit". The gun crew were very het up, they had never fired at a tank before. While it came even closer I looked through the sights. The tank had obviously not considered us to be an important target and was only shooting on the off-chance that it was a likely enemy position. Feldwebel Zeigler could no longer contain himself. His order to fire was lost in a reverberating crash. A huge dust cloud in front of the gun muzzle and over on the "Bandit" a

burst of flame from the turret and then a series of explosions. My men jumped with joy and slapped each other on the back. We needed this victory, now the whole company was in high spirits and I had difficulty keeping them under cover. Quickly I had a tarpaulin put over the muzzle of the PAK to cut down the huge cloud of dust that the firing had caused.

'I couldn't believe my eyes, I thought at first that we had knocked out a lone tank, but then from all sides more tanks appeared through the haze. We couldn't stop them alone – I counted over 20 tanks, but I didn't recognise their types. They stopped about 1,800 metres away. Twenty-five tanks against my company with one PAK, two machine guns and one heavy machine gun. The second company lay in echelon 500 metres to our right rear and the third in reserve behind Company HQ. On the left I had no support. Of our own tanks there was absolutely nothing to be seen. We could never destroy this superior force, but to retreat over the overhang was equally impossible, no one would reach the crest of the dune. And from

the heights the British could control all the positions both near and far. I wrote out a rough situation report and asked for tank or artillery support. Then I shivered for a few minutes waiting to be shot or cashiered. As the right wing of the tanks came even nearer to us a runner hurried up with a second man. He was an artillery observer. The three of us lay like sardines in my foxhole. Heaven had sent us this man with the radio. He was excited and shaky and I had to help him to get the correct frequency on his radio. He was also new to Africa, but a cigarette quickly calmed him down. While the Tommies came even closer, he began to give fire orders to his battery. Already I could clearly see the enemy commanders in the turrets of their tanks, I ordered that the PAK should only start to engage at 600 metres. Finally at last a ranging round from the artillery. Too far. Tommy was almost on us. The artillery observer screamed into the microphone: "Defensive fire or it's too late!" Impatiently the PAK crew looked over at me. My heart was in my mouth when I finally ordered them to fire. Suddenly there was a great rushing sound above us. The gunners fired a magnificent salvo right into the middle of the tank concentration. "Excellent!" I yelled into the microphone. One tank had been knocked out and was burning. All the rest, two of which were obviously hit as well, immediately turned around. They managed to pick up a few of the wounded tank crew from the "Bandit" we had hit. I ordered "Cease Fire", but I think anyway that my men wouldn't have shot at the poor devils.

'There now followed salvo after salvo of shells onto our position. Our own artillery had stopped firing as soon as the tanks had turned around, because we had to save ammunition. The observer stayed in my foxhole – that comforted me a lot. The shelling got heavier. Pressed right at the bottom of our foxholes we waited for a direct hit, but clearly such an easy death is only allowed to a lucky few. Aeroplanes came, and I looked up at them with my binoculars, trying to judge when the bombs would come out. We calculated the moment they had to fall to hit us and each time we breathed again when this moment passed, then I would wave to my men that the bombs would miss our position. In the evening there was another tank attack. This time we succeeded in turning it back much earlier through well aimed artillery fire. Until now we had had no losses in this position.

3.9.42

Night passed without incident. Today, on the third anniversary of the British declaration of war, Tommy would want to show his strength. Around us the ground quaked and shook from the artillery shelling. Shrapnel whistled through the air, and again and again sand and stones flew into my foxhole. A self-propelled PAK had taken up position behind us and fired about breakfast time, quickly knocking out three enemy tanks one after another. We "pigmies" in the sand had seemingly become very unimportant, because much more powerful weapons were duelling on our behalf over our heads. The self propelled gun had the enemy artillery fire concentrated on to it and thus had drawn attention away from my position. It was high time that it disappeared rapidly. I suppose that we had become an important strongpoint in the battle. At 1400 I suddenly became aware that a vehicle was coming out of the shimmering foreground. I discovered with my binoculars that it was an enemy scout car that was coming right up to my position. When he was about 150 metres away, he slowly got out and looked at us through his binoculars. He obviously wasn't clear about the extent of our position. We could remedy that. The car had a sun visor erected and the

Left: 'They shall not pass!' Men of the Scots Guards man the El Alamein positions, only 40 miles from Alexandria and Cairo./*IWM*

Below, far left: A German engineer removes a British anti-tank mine, July 1942./*IWM*

Below, centre: 'Dig in'. After unsuccessfully trying to break through the British positions at El Alamein, Rommel was forced to withdraw and to dig in between the sea and the Quattara Depression. The position was of great depth and heavily protected with extensive minefields./*IWM*

Below: 'The throw for Alex'. Rommel made his final thrust for the Canal in the battle of Alam Halfa, 30 August 1942. Two days later he was forced to pull back his forces and to dig in himself. /*IWM*

whole situation was farcical. Had we really camouflaged our position so well that the Tommy had to practically drive into it before he could see us? Or was there so much glare that he simply couldn't see us at all? We aimed at the comical vehicle with one of the machine guns and directed some short bursts of fire at it. The Englishman threw himself down and snaked his way back to his shot up car. He crawled behind it. We couldn't see him properly because of the glare, so he managed to escape.

'During the next barrage I was wounded in my knee by a piece of shrapnel but it didn't hurt for the moment. The company was exhausted and I had to use all my willpower to stop them from falling asleep. Continual observation in the grilling sun rapidly made one tired and started ones' eyes weeping. I had given orders that each heavy weapon must have at least one person on watch, but again and again I discovered a group where all men were asleep. Then we realised that we had nothing left to drink. I could hardly speak any more. Our hopes were concentrated on the evening. God willing, we would then get water and rations and would be able to continue to hold out. I heard from battalion that our tanks had stopped through lack of petrol. There was much talk of treachery. I had the feeling that the dream of Cairo had faded and that we would be unable to repeat it because we had over extended ourselves. In the evening the first big shock of my army career – our first retreat. We had had no enemy pressure. There was great confusion – people shouting, giving orders, replying, threatening, if retreat was inevitable then it should take place calmly, that would have been better. But in the last few days nerves had frayed. Because there was insufficient room on the vehicles the Chief said we would have to get the heavy machine gun group to walk to the new position 10 kilometres away. Depressed, I thought that even we had received ridiculous orders. In the pitch black night the Chief sent for me. The weight of his responsibility had allowed him no rest. He ordered me to find the PAK gun tower that was lying a few kilometres behind and the heavy machine gun group. Our last vehicles had passed us – even the tank rearguard. How should I find these men and the tower in this darkness? I lay on the front mudguard of my vehicle with my eyes only a few centimetres above the ground and only like that could I see tank trackmarks and tell the driver which way to go. One man held onto my feet. Suddenly an earpiercing explosion and hot water gushed all over me – the radiator had burst! Here in no man's land and only three men with me. We shouted and heard voices. We were lucky. Only 50 metres away from us stood the fully laden tower with the PAK. The heavy machine gun group was also there. . . .'

After a thoroughly unpleasant night wandering around in no man's land in the pitch darkness, during which time they bumped into a party of British, Lt Ringler managed to guide his men back to rejoin the battalion and to reach their new defensive position.

This rebuff at Alam Halfa marked a turning point in the fortunes of the Afrika Korps. Having failed in his gamble to break through the British lines and strike for Cairo and Alexandria, Rommel decided to withdraw. The British did not follow up, General Montgomery sensibly deciding that he had first to build up his strength. The Axis troops dug in and began to prepare their own defensive positions in great depth, between the Mediterranean and the Quattara Depression. Rommel, shortly afterwards, had to report sick for the very first time in his life (apart from when wounded) and flew back to Germany for treatment.

Off Duty

Off Duty Entertainment

Like soldiers of any nation when in a strange land far from home, the men of the DAK were determined to make the most of what little leisure time was available to them. Mostly this was in the form of all too brief days out of action, with little or no chance of reaching even semi-civilisation. Consequently, their amusements had to be self-generated as the photographs in this section show. For those who were able to visit Tripoli or one of the other large towns, then the types of entertainment available were more varied. I have tried to cover as many off duty pursuits as possible, but, as one might expect, wine, women and song were clearly the most popular!

'Darling Lilli'

Probably the most famous song in the last war was the still popular 'Lilli Marlene' ('Lili Marleen' in the original German version). How avidly the troops on both sides listened on their radio sets to the story of her patient vigil under the street lamp outside her lover's barracks. So it would be unthinkable to produce a book about the Desert War without mentioning her. I have been very fortunate in getting permission from Derek Jewell, to reproduce his excellent article entitled *A Song for All Armies,* which first appeared in 1967, in the *Sunday Times/Sphere* paperback *Alamein and the Desert War,* which he edited. I was also lucky enough to be able to contact Norbert Schultze who wrote the original haunting melody. He has very kindly given me some up-to-date information on that 'little girl Lili Marleen' as he fondly calls her. It is clear that her popularity is undimmed and she remains as firm a favourite as 'Tipperary' or 'Pack up your Troubles' from World War I.

A Song for All Armies

'Every three months a plump statement of account plops through the door of Norbert Schultze's house in West Berlin. It lists the not insubstantial sums in royalties which still accrue to him from "Lilli Marlene" ("Lili Marleen" in the original German) for

Below: Spillikins. At the time of El Alamein the DAK were very short of entertainment so some enterprising divisions managed to obtain quantities of games for the troops to play when off duty. */IWM*

which he wrote the music. In the first quarter of 1967 recordings of the song were played, according to the account, in Austria, Canada, Australia, Japan, New Zealand, the USA (several hundred dollars worth of royalties) the UAR (a mere 17 pfennigsworth), Holland, Spain, Belgium, Norway, France, Denmark, Greece, Italy, Sweden, Switzerland, Peru, West Germany, Britain and a score of other countries. "Lilli Marlene" has lasted well. Twenty-five years ago it had a similar world-wide appeal, though Schultze was not at that time collecting the proceeds. Royalties from the song were withheld from him by the Custodians of Enemy Property in various countries for many years after the war too. Only in the last 15 years has he received the full rewards. He estimates the song has brought him in around £50,000 – and for this he owes a great deal to the combined offensives of the Afrika Korps and 8th Army. Before they stepped in, the odds against "Lilli Marlene" becoming virtually the only memorable song to emerge from the 1939-45 war were ludicrously long. The poem which inspired it was written, and half-forgotten, by a German soldier called Hans Leip, in 1917. When 20 years later, the words were set by Norbert Schultze to the tune we know – which was by no means the first – the song was hawked around 30 German publishers before it was unenthusiastically accepted. The first record of it made in 1939 by Lale Andersen, daughter of a shipwright, born in Bremerhaven, sold 700 copies. Then it was forgotten. Even when it burst out of obscurity, by accident, in 1941, it was nearly buried again. Goebbels hated it so much he

Top: A game of chess in progress, using bullets of various calibres and Verey cartridges to take the place of missing chessmen. */Bundesarchiv, Koblenz*

Above: The Entertainment Officer of 21 Panzer Division rustled up eight accordians for issue to units about the time of El Alamein. */Bundesarchiv, Kobenz*

Right: Newspapers and magazines from home, such as this hunting magazine, were eagerly read by everyone./*Bundesarchiv, Koblenz*

Left: A conjurer entertains, pulling out a string of razor blades from his mouth./*Bundesarchiv, Koblenz*

Right: A battery sing song in 190 Artillerie Regiment./*W. Susek*

Below right: Everyone enjoyed swimming in the sparkling waters of the Mediterranean, but a sentry always had to remain on the alert./*IWM*

Below: A novel mobile band visiting 190 Artillerie Regiment. Bands were very difficult to get as were all forms of entertainment, but some did manage to get up to the front line./*W. Susek*

ordered one of the two master matrices to be destroyed; the other, fortunately, was in London. The authorities in Britain weren't very keen on the song either. It was, after all, German. And the woman in the song seemed to be – well, some sort of trollop, wasn't she? So they said anyway, maybe for propaganda reasons. But at least they didn't ban it, unlike an American war music committee, which believed it would harm soldier morale. Equally oddly, this is a song whose sense demands that it be sung by a man. Yet the notable recorded versions among the many dozens made of it have always been women – from Lale Andersen, through Anne Shelton, Vera Lynn and Marlene Dietrich, to Connie Francis. Nobody associates it with Bing Crosby or Hank Snow or the Band of the Coldstream Guards or a pianist called Honky van Tonk, all of whom also recorded it. Perhaps the biggest piece of luck which both Schultze and Lale Andersen had was that her record of "Lili Marleen" was lying with a few others in a cellar in Vienna during the summer of 1941. Radio stations for Axis propaganda were being set up, and in Belgrade a studio was prepared to beam programmes to the *Panzerarmee Afrika*. The station had an announcer and a whole wad of news and propaganda – but no records. A

soldier was sent to Vienna to find some. There have been many claimants to the role of the war's most inspired pop-picker. Not even Schultze knows for sure who did him the favour – but he thinks it was a corporal named Kistenmacher. Frankly, Kistenmacher hadn't much choice in that cellar. He brought back to Belgrade the handful of records he found. An officer played them over and liked the bugle-call intro which had been written for Lale Andersen's "Lilli" by her accompanist. He thought it would be great as close-down music. Radio Belgrade played it first on 18 August 1941. Within a week there were several thousand requests (demands, rather) from German soldiers in North Africa for it to be played again. Soon it became a fixture on Radio Belgrade at 9.55 pm – the last record of the night. On only three nights in the next three years was the soft and haunting air not heard – immediately following the smashing of the German armies in Stalingrad, when Goebbels banned entertainment of any sort. From 1941 to 1944 a dozen German stations were playing it up to 30 times daily.

'But, ironically, the whole world was soon singing it. Within a year it had become World War II's classic. Eighth Army quickly picked it up in the Western Desert, partly

Above: Stuka pilots in Cyrenaica enjoying a swim in the Mediterranean.
/*Bundesarchiv, Koblenz*

Left: There's nothing like messing around in boats, even rubber ones./*Brig P. A. L. Vaux*

Above right: 'Nacktkultur' on the beach. Of course swimming costumes were hardly ever necessary or available!/*W. Susek*

Centre right: Swimming party at Bardia. This was the first swim for over two months for these artillery men./*W. Susek*

Below right: The magnificent bathing beach at Bardia. /*W. Susek*

from their radios, partly from Axis prisoners. It became a song for marching to, a song for sitting down to – the property of virtually every nation engaged in the war. From German soldiers, Lale Andersen received an estimated 1,000,000 fan letters, usually addressed to "Lili Marleen", during the first year or so after the song crept onto the air. Versions of it in many languages were written. The first verse in the German version, roughly translated, went: "In front of the barracks, before the heavy gate, there stood a lamp post, and it still stands there. Let's hope we meet again there and stand beneath the lamp as we used to do, Lili Marleen". The message was given an idio-syncratic twist by every nation which pro-vided lyrics. For the Italians, one verse (undiscoverable in the original) began "Give me a rose, and press it to my heart". The French ("*Et dans la nuit sombre nos corps enlaces*") disguised nothing. The English went squarely down the middle.

"Underneath the lantern
By the barrack gate
Darling I remember
The way you used to wait:
'Twas there that you whispered tenderly,
That you loved me,
You'd always be
My Lilli of the lamplight
My own Lilli Marlene."

The man who wrote those words, Tommie Connor, is a lyricist who has had around

39

Above: Outside the Benghazi
cinema./*IWM*

Peaches for Africa

Photographs: PK. war correspondent Kenneweg (4)

Prize crew. The wreck was discovered by soldiers belonging to a German reconnaissance tank unit looking for a bathing place after a gruelling run. The hatches were unbroken and the cargo undamaged. The first sample of the booty is brought to land in an inflatable boat

Flotsam and jetsam. An Italian submarine sank this cargo-boat travelling in a convoy in the Mediterranean. It broke into two parts. The wind slowly drove the front part of the ship towards the south until it stranded. Now it lies in one of the countless deserted bays on the coast of Cyrenaika

Working leave. The fortunate men who discovered the wreck are given "leave." For six days they row enthusiastically to and from the wreck. By then they have landed their find and conveyed it to their base

The tasty contents. The German soldiers now enjoy what was intended for the British troops in Alexandria: wine, whisky, cigarettes and countless tins of Californian peaches which are particularly enjoyable in the great heat

3,000 songs published. "I saw Mummy Kissing Santa Claus", "It's my Mother's Birthday Today", "Who's Taking You Home Tonight?" and "Under the Spreading Chestnut Tree" were some of them. " 'Lilli Marlene' is far from my favourite song", he said in the summer of 1967. "Frankly, I took it as a work of propaganda. I was rung up in 1942 and told that the BBC and the Government were desperate for a lyric that would go to the hearts of people. There had been a lot of controversy over the song, which was being sung out in the desert to amateurish lyrics which were, to put it bluntly, dirty and risqué. I knew about the German version, but I couldn't use that. Wasn't it all about a young prostitute who wanted to give as much for her country as the soldiers – so she gave her body. Can you imagine that in English? I had to write a song imagining the girl was a daughter, a mother, sister or sweetheart – a song that wouldn't offend the hearts and morals of people. Honestly, I was stumped – so I said a prayer, and the lyric was finished in 25 minutes Anne Shelton made the first record of it in Britain and it sold a million".

'Parodies of the song abounded in every language, as every soldier in the Western Desert well knew. These were, of course the true ballads of the war, usually cynical in tone, and often bawdy. One desert version of "Lili" had a refrain which went "We're off to Bomb Benghazi, we're off to bomb BG" but the best known emerged after the Desert War when 8th Army, fighting a slow, foul and bitter war in Italy, heard a rumour that a woman politician back in England had referred to them as "D-Day Dodgers". They reacted like this:

Top: I never did find out what the competition was all about, but I certainly like the prizes! /*Brig P. A. L. Vaux*

Above: Prosit! A gaunt faced Rommel joins some German sailors in a toast to the Fatherland./*K. Popplewell*

Left: A page out of the German propaganda magazine *Signal* (Edition No 21 of November 1941), published here by kind permission of the Imperial War Museum./*Eileen Tweedy*

Right: Soldiers' Club, Derna. /*Brig P. A. L. Vaux*

Above: A field artillery battery hold an impromptu party whilst in a reserve area./*W. Susek*

Left: Signing on the dotted line. Another proxy marriage taking place in the desert. The wedding bouquets are nice, but alas, the bride is miles away./*IWM*

Above right: Proxy wedding. It was possible for soldiers to marry at long distance such as this very young looking prospective bridegroom – poor chap, I bet he had a rotten honeymoon all on his own!
/*Bundesarchiv, Koblenz*

Centre right: 5 Panzer Regiment Recreational Club, Apollonia, Libya, May 1942.
/*Bundesarchiv, Koblenz*

Below right: A shady patio, plus band, is an ideal way to pass a pleasant afternoon.
/*Bundesarchiv, Koblenz*

"We're the D-Day Dodgers, out in Italy –
Always on the vino, always on the spree.
Eighth Army scroungers and their tanks
We live in Rome, among the Yanks.
We are the D-Day Dodgers, way out in Italy."

There were far more sombre overtones to other parodies, however. In Denmark and Norway one ran: "In front of the barracks, beside the heavy gate, there stands the lamp post, but now it is too late. Who is it I see hanging there? A little man, with wayward hair. You know, Lili Marleen, you know Lili Marleen". In all such parody versions, "Lilli Marlene" was the undoubted successor to "Mademoiselle from Armentieres". But it was the straight version which, along with the carol, "Silent Night", was heard along *both* front lines as the Germans and the men of 8th Army wearily faced each other across the mud and snow of Italy at Christmas 1943. It was the same version which, some time later, WAAFs near London were forbidden to sing within earshot of German POWs – because it might lead to fraternisation.

'About 250 women like to think they were the original Lili Marleen, according to Hans Leip, the poet. He was a fusilier in the Kaiser's army, and while he was on an officers' course in Berlin he got involved with two girls. One was Lili (real name Betty, the greengrocer's daughter downstairs), the other Marleen, a doctor's daughter whom he picked up in an art gallery. Lili was really a friend's girl, but one night on his way to sentry duty she begged him "Stay, stay". With Marleen, a part-time nurse he was much more involved. The same night of Lili's invitation, Leip was on guard duty. It was rainy, the street lamp glowed on the wet pavement. Then Marleen passed by, in feather boa. She said "Bye-bye, so long". Later, on an iron bed in the guard room, Leip wrote his poem. "My thoughts clung anxiously to the forms of the two girls, as though one were not enough to engage fate to bring me safely home", he has said. "Their names could no longer be coupled together with an 'and'. They melted into one, not too shapely, as a single pleasure and pain".

'The poem that Leip wrote is a sad touching piece: "A private little love-song", he calls it. Why the general idea that the woman was a prostitute (which is the least of several fantastic versions of the genesis of the Lili original) is unclear. Was the notion encouraged by Allied propagandists who instinctively disliked the notion of a German song becoming the rage? Leip is mystified that the idea should have taken root in England. "They were both very proper girls", he says. And his verses are a straightforward love story, about the sadness of parting in wartime. The last stanza is metaphysical in tone. The man sees himself dead

45

("in earthly depths, my dear") and returning to meet the girl under the lamp as a ghost. But in 1917 there was no literary mystery. Leip went to the front and never saw the girls again. The poem was, ultimately, published in an anthology of Leip's works. Sales were modest. Norbert Schultze first heard about "Lili Marleen" in 1938. He was a young composer of light music making his way in Berlin. He was working on his first movie score (Moroccan Romance). He had recently had his children's opera, Black Peter, performed. A tenor in the chorus asked Schultze to turn out some songs for his radio jobs – and handed over the Leip book. Schultze set 10 of the poems to music, but the tenor didn't like Lili Marleen. "Today he is still angry not to have sung it" says Schultze, now a well-preserved sixtyish, with a shock of grey hair. So he gave it one day to Lale Andersen, whom he had known around the cabarets of Berlin and Munich for several years. "In those days she had a dreary, moaning voice. But she looked marvellous. Blonde hair, white sweater, white teeth. I liked her".

'Lale Andersen didn't care much for Schultze's work either. She already had another composer's version of "Lili Marleen" in her repertoire. But she sang both versions in clubs to see how they went, and the audiences preferred the marching rhythm of Schultze's tune, so she stuck to that. She sang it once on Radio Cologne in 1939, then put the song on record – the first she had ever made. But its sentiment was against the tide of feeling in Hitler's Germany. Much more martial, nationalistic, rabble rousing airs were in demand. "Lili Marleen" sank out of sight. But if his tune was quickly forgotten,

Above: It was very difficult for the Army to get 'live shows' in the desert as the Luftwaffe could always offer much better accommodation! This native band and singers appear to be performing in a fairly substantial building – perhaps in Tripoli or Tunis?/*Bundesarchiv, Koblenz*

then Schultze was not. Unknown to him, he had been placed on the Nazi list of creative artists who would be excused military service. They were needed to hymn the achievements of the New Order at war. Towards the end of 1939 he received his first commission: the music for *Baptism of Fire*, a propaganda documentary about Poland. "For the first time", Schultze recalls, "I saw the horror of war. The bombing of Warsaw, the holes in the houses. I thought, my God, I feel sorry for these people. What can I write? The Air Ministry people said there would be a voice coming out of heaven saying 'For all this misery, all this horror, you will have to bear responsibility, Mr Chamberlain'. I thought that only a solemn march like 'Eroica' would do. So that's what I wrote". Schultze, richer by £150 for his first propaganda score, was now launched on his wartime career. Soon Hitler wanted a song about the new enemy: Schultze turned out "*Bomben auf Engelland*". In the next four years or so he wrote 25 war songs to order – "Songs of the Nation", as the Germans called them – including "*Panzer rollen in Afrika vor*". And in 1941, when the demand was for a song to go with total war in Russia, Schultze turned out "*Führer Befiehl*" – with Goebbel's help. Beside all this, the sudden success of "Lili Marleen" in late 1941 seemed to the Nazi bosses, and even to Schultze, almost incidental. But it impressed Rommel enough for him to send an officer, laden with boxes of coffee and brandy, to see Schultze. Could he compose a song for Rommel? "I could scarcely refuse", says Schultze. The result, recorded by the Luftwaffe orchestra, was called "Forward with Rommel". "But by the time I'd finished it, Rommel was going

backwards, so it was never used". Schultze knew nothing about the resurgence of "Lili Marleen" until friends told him it was being played on Radio Belgrade. The first that Lale Andersen knew about it was when she began to receive letters addressed to "Lili Marleen, Radio Belgrade, Berlin, Germany". She had been singing, relatively unsensationally, in German clubs. Suddenly, everyone wanted her. And if the troops couldn't get her, they settled for Schultze and his wife Iva Vanya, the Bulgarian-born actress he married in 1941.

' "I made some money from the record", says Lale Andersen, "but my life didn't change much because of the war. I had the whole world before me, but I couldn't enjoy it". Her life, in fact, swiftly changed for the worse. Goebbels became very interested in the woman who meant so much to the Afrika Korps and who sang a song of which he disapproved strongly. He discovered that prewar she had acted in plays directed by Rolf Liebermann, a Jew. She seemed still to be friendly with Liebermann, who was in Zurich. So though she sang for troops in Germany and other occupied countries, beady eyes were watching her. In 1942, she travelled to Italy to sing to wounded German soldiers and was unwise enough to write to Liebermann asking for the addresses of people who might help her to get to Zurich, via Milan. The Gestapo intercepted the letter and she was brought back to Berlin. "They told me it was the end of my career, that I would be sent away to a camp. The night after that interview I thought, I'll finish the whole thing. I took all the sleeping pills I had. It was three weeks before I knew anything. I expected the Gestapo to finish me

off. But a British broadcast saved me. The BBC put out a report that I'd been taken to a concentration camp and died. Goebbels saw it as a golden opportunity to prove that the English radio told lies. He needed me alive. He put out a broadcast that I wasn't dead, but that I'd been very ill, that I couldn't sing again for a long time. They didn't send me to a camp, but I had to report to the Gestapo twice a week".

'Lale Andersen stayed in Berlin until 1944. The Gestapo seemed slowly to lose interest in her. One night she slipped away to Langeroog, a small island in the North Sea where her grandparents lived. There she remained until the war was nearly over. For Lale Andersen, the end of the war meant the resumption of a career, which, though never world shattering, was underwritten by her wartime fame. In 1945 the British Forces Network in Germany invited her to sing at the Musikhalle in Hamburg. There followed years of tours in Europe, America, Britain; a film based on the song which featured Lale in 1952, a steady flow of records, many of whose songs today sound strangely outdated. In the spring of 1967 Lale Andersen was back in Hamburg's Musikhalle, still slim and blonde, with a pink mink and dark glasses, in her fifties, on her final farewell tour. She sang, of course, "Lili Marleen" in a sad sort of whine, after introducing it as "my fateful song" to an audience of the faithful, very middle aged, 500 in number in a hall that can seat 2,000. The past seemed alive for them. After almost every number someone rushed on stage to give her flowers. "Five thousand, 10,000, 20,000 times I have sung it", she said afterwards. "Who knows. I am never tired of it. The lyric is never routine. It is too strong and too good".

48

'For the other two people who created the most popular song in German history, peace was rather different. In 1967, Hans Leip was still a poet and novelist, living in Switzerland. In 1945 he lived near Innsbruck. One evening when Eisenhower was visiting US troops there he asked to see Leip. At the time, Leip says he was sleeping – because, according to the locals, he had been going to bed before 10pm for years to avoid having to listen to "Lili Marleen" on Radio Belgrade. Eisenhower, Leip says, ordered that he was not to be disturbed, "because he's the only German who has given pleasure to the world during the war". Norbert Schultze and his wife were trapped in Berlin as the Russians blasted their way into it. Sometimes he hid in attics, at others he sang with his wife at Russian concerts; twice he was pushed into a detention camp. Finally they managed to move to the American Zone in Berlin, where they began entertaining at officers' clubs. In December 1945, an officer invited them to come and sing Lili at a dinner which Montgomery was attending. "So Iva and I sang it. In French, German, English. I can still see him sitting there. Perhaps he thought of all that this song meant. But it seemed to make no impression on him. He clapped, got up and went away. Later in the evening a British war correspondent came up and asked me hadn't I written *"Bomben auf Engelland"*? Next day there were newspaper reports about how I had wormed my way in to sing in front of Montgomery. There were very anti, very terrible stories. I was called up to the OSS office and told I was on the black list. I was not to be allowed to perform".

'For two years Schultze worked as a labourer – on building sites, in gardens. In 1948 he moved to his hometown, Brunswick, and slowly picked up the threads of being a composer again. He was officially "denazified", though even today Berlin papers call him a "Nazi composer". He is now modestly successful, writing operas, film and television music. "I can't", said Schultze in 1967, "regret that I wrote all those war songs. It was the time that governed it, not me. Other people shot, I made songs. Our enemy in those days was England. What was I supposed to do? I composed with a clear conscience. But I can understand how people feel today. They remember they had to sit in shelters and listen to my marches on the radio and now they say 'My God, that's the man who composed all those bloody marches'. They don't sing 'Lili Marleen' anywhere much in Germany today. . . . When did we last sing it, Iva? Maybe 1951? It's all past. In Germany it's associated with the war and it's all unpleasant. Maybe a pianist in a bar will play it around one in the morning when a group of old officers full of beer demand it. Then with

49

‘Lili Marleen’

NACH GEDÍCHTEN
VON
HANS LEIP
MUSIK:
NORBERT SCHULTZE

Above: Lale Andersen, the original singer of 'Lili Marleen', arriving at Northolt Airport on 21 March 1950 on her first visit to England./*Keystone Press*

Above left: 'Lili Marleen'. This is the original cover of the first edition piano score of the five songs from Hans Leip's *Kleine Hafenorgel* published in 1940 by Apollo-Verlag. There were only 1,000 copies, all hand coloured. (Reproduced by kind permission of Peter Maurice Music Co Ltd, 138-140 Charing Cross Road, London WC2H OLD)./*A. Atkins*

Left: A street scene in Tripoli. Note the splendid cloak (*Umhang*) worn by the officer in the foreground./*Col T. Bock*

Right: Norbert Schultze, composer of the haunting ' Lili Marleen' melody, is still hard at work as a musical director in Hamburg. /*Norbert Schultze*

LILLI MARLENE
(Pronounced "LILY MARLANE")

Words and Music by

Tune Uke G.C.E.A.
*Accordion

HANS LEIP
NORBERT SCHULTZE
& TOMMIE CONNOR

Right: 'Lilli Marlene'. The story of how the English words came to be written was thus: 'In a pub in Stoke Poges, publisher Jimmy Phillips is having a game of darts with Bandleader Billy Cotton when in bursts a bunch of boisterous soldiers, and almost immediately they break into "Lilli Marlene" – in German. Just for a joke Jimmy Phillips says "Better be careful with that song boys, or we'll have the village copper here arresting you as enemy spies". Their officer approaches Jimmy and, rather close, says through clenched teeth, "Look here, this is our song! This is the song we hear on our radios in our tanks in the North African desert. Mouth organs strike up 'Lilli' at night. We sing it in day charges against the Germans. 'Lilli Marlene' gets us right in our guts. 'Lilli Marlene' is the theme song of the desert war and get that straight!" Quick as a wink Jimmy says, "Why don't you get some English lyrics then?". The officer sings him six English versions but Jimmy finds they all stink. Back in London, Jimmy and lyricist Tommie Connor brought the German poem down to earth. "As far as I could see", says Jimmy, "the German song was about a barracks tart that this soldier dreams about. He sees her coming down to him in the trenches enveloped in a regular lust cloud. All that's a bit poetic, so we put in some lamplight scenes and made the song more accessible".'
(Reproduced by permission of Peter Maurice Music Co Ltd, 138-140 Charing Cross Road, London WC2H 0LD)/*A. Atkins*

a bad conscience he plays it – but he hates it"'.

As I have explained that article was written in 1967. Since then Norbert Schultze has moved to Hamburg where he was recently the musical director of 'Black Fair' (*Schwarzer Fahrmarkt*) a successful musical about the Berlin of 1945-47. He sent me details of the substantial quarterly royalties which he still receives for 'Lili' from as far afield as Japan, South Africa, Australia, and Brazil. In 1972 his son, Norbert junior, produced and directed a TV documentary about the song which he had filmed all over the world. He also mentioned rumours of another film in the offing. More recently, the song was played during Monty's funeral ceremonies. Like the memory of that great old soldier, so too the memory of 'Lilli Marlene' will remain with us for many, many years to come.

Supply

The First Essential

'The first essential condition for an army to be able to stand the strain of battle is an adequate stock of weapons, petrol and ammunition. In fact, the battle is fought and decided by the quartermasters before the shooting begins. The bravest men can do nothing without guns, the guns nothing without plenty of ammunition, and neither guns nor ammunition are of much use in mobile warfare unless there are vehicles, with sufficient petrol to haul them around. Maintenance must also approximate, both in quantity and quality, to that available to the enemy'.*

So wrote Rommel after losing at El Alamein – 'the decisive battle of the African campaign' as he rightly called it. Rommel put into words what must have been all too clear to those who fought in Africa, but could not or would not be appreciated by the German High

The Rommel Papers Ed B. H. Liddell Hart.

Command. I would add one more item to the short list of essentials he mentions namely water, perhaps the most precious of all commodities in the desert. Later in this section we shall look at the problem of water supply in more detail, through the eyes of a German photographer who followed the progress of a water can in North Africa. Before doing so we should understand the vital and fundamental part which supply played in the course of the war in Africa. Major-General J. F. C. Fuller, CB, CBE, DSO in his book *Decisive Battles of the Western World* likened the situation in Libya to a piece of elastic. The line of supply for either army could be safely stretched about 300 to 400 miles from its main base – Tripoli for the Germans, Alexandria for the British – however, if either side tried to stretch the elastic further, before intermediate bases could be established, then it would snap and the penalty was 'a gallop back to avoid annihilation'. When the Germans reached El Alamein for example, it took a convoy seven days to complete the

Below: The Afrika Korps advances during Rommel's counter-attack January 1942. The tanks, half tracks and heavy lorries seen in this photograph could only be kept moving with a continuous supply of petrol, ammunition and the other necessities of war./*IWM*

round trip from Benghazi, at a constant speed of 40 miles per hour, and two weeks to get to Tripoli and back!

The Supplies Must Get Through!

In this section I have chosen three photographic stories all taken from the German military propaganda magazine *Signal*, which have supply as their main topic. One I have already mentioned – the water can. The second deals with the passage of a supply column through the desert and is called *The Desert Novice and other matters of interest concerning the vital supply service in Africa*. The pictures and their captions tell the story extremely well, although the *Desert Novice* does not play quite as large a part in the proceedings as his top billing might suggest!

Travels of a Water Can

Juan Iversen Thomae writes:

'In Africa WATER is written in capital letters. Whoever wages war there needs water above all. Drinking water and water in the radiators of the motors. Tanks, anti-tank guns, AA guns, reinforcements, all of them are motorised and all of them need water. The only thing that can run in the desert without water is that little masterpiece, the People's Car. It is a matter of course, therefore, that all conversation turns round three things: water, petrol and ammunition. If there is no water the advance is held up, therefore water must be found. There are wells, waterholes and the sea; then there are distilling plants, both portable and stationary. As can be expected, the retreating enemy

Top: Resupply column. Volkswagens, cross-country cars and lorries, belonging to 21 Panzer Division, moving up towards the front line January 1942./*IWM*

Above: Supplies from Europe. A shipload of lorries, crammed with supplies, runs the gauntlet through the Mediterranean. The lorries carrying the large drums of fuel are 8 tonner Tatras. Note the life rafts ready for speedy launching. /*Brig P. A. L. Vaux*

Right: A Volkswagen Kfz 1 churns through soft sand. This splendid little vehicle was used for a wide variety of tasks and was much prized by both sides in the desert war. /*German Armour School*

53

destroys all waterholes, wells, distilling apparatuses and pumps; he blows them up, batters them to pieces, dismantles them and buries parts far below the surface of the desert. When the advance begins, the troops bring a certain supply of water with them, but not enough for marches of hundreds of miles such as are made by Field Marshal Rommel. Water must be found, drawn and distributed among the troops so that the soldier can drink and the radiators can be filled. The Afrika Korps is accompanied by numerous water columns, each one of these water columns is equipped with a portable water pump that can be set up in a minimum of time and is fitted with an overhead tank and tapping point etc, enabling lorries and separate water cans to be filled very soon after the pump has been fixed up. Considering the great demand for water during big advances, every increase in pumping plants is welcome. Separate commandos are sent out to look for spare parts or suitable material from which additional emergency plants can be erected. Strange as it may seem, the desert can supply everything one requires of it. But one must know how to look for it. Somewhere or other damaged or dented water tanks can be found which, with a certain amount of skill, can be welded together again. It is easy to find thirty, fifty or even a few hundred feet of water piping somewhere which can be bent, cut and repaired in the workshop of the water supply company. Pumps can be found, whole pumps, half pumps and pieces of pumps; valves can be found, cylinders and gear-wheels, all as if by magic. Two or three little pumps can do the work of one big pump. One day after the capture of Mersa Matruh I met a lieutenant-colonel with a wheel on his shoulder strap (an engineer), a quiet cultured scholar. He was the com-

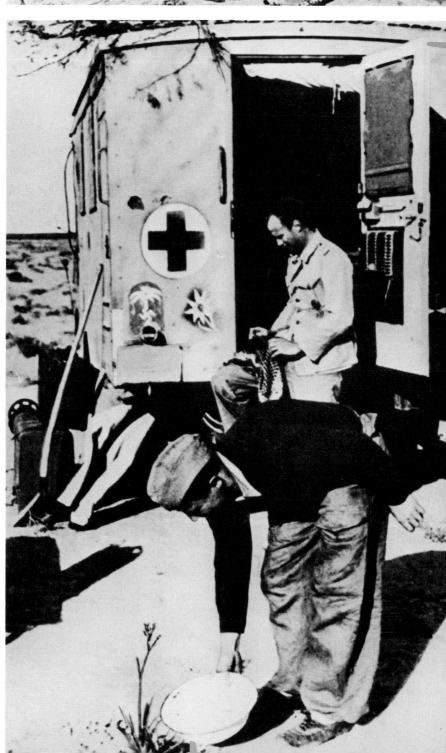

Far left: The 15 Panzer Division sign is clearly visible on the mudguard of this supply vehicle. /*H. Long*

Left: Fitters deal with a tricky repair on a Volkswagen car in their open air workshop. /*Col T. Bock*

Below left: The crew of this ambulance must be keen gardeners to use precious washing water on their 'garden'!/*Col T. Bock*

Right: Fresh meat, such as this gazelle, must have made quite a change from the interminable tins of 'alter Mann'./*Col T. Bock*

Below: Prosit! One of the nicest forms of booty – a bottle of Black Horse ale disappearing fast!/*Bundesarchiv, Koblenz*

mander of the water supply company of the Afrika Korps. While I chatted with him in the district commander's office, the word "water" was bandied about on all sides. Twelve miles east of Mersa Matruh was a camp of 4,000 British prisoners who had to be provided with drinking water. The lieutenant-colonel remained quite unruffled. "My men have already found water. But there remains the question of transport. As you know, all the lorries are urgently needed during an advance".

"How do you know that water is to be found at a certain place and above all how do you pump it? How do you run it off into cans and casks? How do you forward it to the troops?"

'Quietly and objectively he began to talk. It could be assumed that the British had enough water, from waterholes, wells or distillation plants. They had to be found and put in order once more. Sometimes this was rather difficult, for the British were very clever at polluting with chemicals. The work of his water supply company consisted first of all in finding the water, secondly in purifying and thirdly in distributing it. The wells which have not been blown up or hopelessly contaminated by the British are purified by special chemical processes. Each column has its own chemists. In the desert large quantities of water are obtained by means of the so-called filter galleries, a kind of covered ditch. They can be cut most conveniently among the dunes and here the water engineer's talent for finding fresh water without letting salt water trickle in is put to the test. Strange to say the best drinking water in the desert is found near the coast. As often as he can, sometimes every hour, the chemist tests the water that is trickling in for salt with a special apparatus when he has it but if, as in Mersa Matruh, it has been smashed by a British bomb, he does so by tasting. Last of all there are water-holes and proper wells. They are not, however, the kind of wells in which the water bubbles out of the earth like a real spring. It collects at a depth of many feet, sometimes quickly, sometimes slowly and has to be brought to the surface by means of pumps. As soon as the water plant has been conjured up, as if by magic, in the desert by this quiet lieutenant-colonel's water supply company, a plain little wooden notice appears by the roadside on which a hastily scribbled word can be seen. Every column and lorry driver, every officer and man is eagerly on the look-out for it; it is the alpha and omega of an advance in Africa and strange to say, it was always to be found on the way from Derna to El Alamein; *Water 200 yards!*'

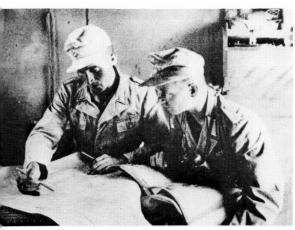

Above left: Final instructions are given by the adjutant of the OC divisional supply service to the commander of the convoy which has been given the task of taking the supplies up to the front.

Left: At 5am the next day the dispatch riders receive their orders. They will have to maintain contact with columns numbering 100 lorries over distances of 60-120 miles through the desert.

Below left: Meanwhile the lorries are loaded from small dumps widely

distributed as added protection from air attack.

Bottom left: Tank reinforcements for El Alamein overtake the convoy.

Above: Men watching for enemy planes sit on the mudguards of every vehicle. When planes are spotted the convoy will spread out to reduce the possibility of damage.

Below: 'Alert.' The convoy leader has sighted a formation of bombers.

Left: Men of an artillery unit eat a hasty snack during a halt in the desert. /*W. Susek*

Left: A large number of bombs explode amongst our lorries and, unfortunately, kill one man and wound five others. Three lorries are damaged and must be abandoned.

Above left: His burial simple and unostentatious – soon the desert will have smoothed out everything and only a piece of plank will reveal that a German soldier fell here.

Above right: The operation on a severely wounded man is carried out in the **ambulance car.**

The Desert Novice
This series of photographs and their captions are taken from the German propaganda magazine *Signal* (Edition No 20 of October 1942) and are published here by kind permission of the Imperial War Museum./*Eileen Tweedy*

Above Right: This British fighter had been shot down the day before – smashed to smithereens. We buried the pilot just as we buried our fallen comrades.

Right: 'What is it this time?' A message brought to the convoy leader by the wireless truck can mean a change in the division's position or a new minefield.

Below: Our objective is reached: as the lorries unload the drivers receive rations.

Above right: The desert novice gives himself away. How? By drinking from a beaker – no veteran does that, it means the loss of a few drops of water.

Right: 'Orders carried out, Sir!' Four words, but what personal courage and devotion to duty are required to ensure the front is well supplied.

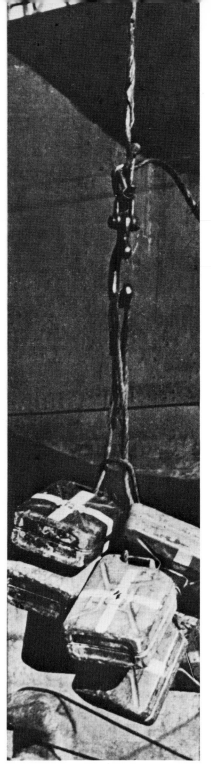

The Travels of Water Can No 4
Taken from the German propaganda magazine *Signal* and published here by kind permission of the Imperial War Museum.
/*Eileen Tweedy*

Left: Water can No 4, arrives on African soil.

Above: At the well, simultaneously with seven others, the can is filled.

Above right: It travels by camel to the front line where thirsty men are waiting.

Right: Well camouflaged, No 4 offers the outposts a welcome drink.

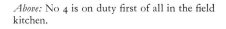

Above: No 4 is on duty first of all in the field kitchen.

Left: On the road to the front, the boiling radiator of our car is refreshed.

Right: The can as a drinking mug – heavy but refreshing.

A Repair Shop One Square Kilometre in Area

Taken from the German propaganda magazine *Signal* (Edition No 18 of 1942) and published here by kind permission of the Imperial War Museum./*Eileen Tweedy*

Above left: Repairs to a motorcycle.

Above: The desert repair shop is protected by twin MGs against low flying attacks by enemy aircraft.

Above right: The soul of this huge repair shop is the big current generator plant which is driven by a diesel engine and supplies the various repair lorries with current by means of long cables.

Right: The men in the desert repair shop are versatile specialists; here they take the engine out of a reconnaissance car for a thorough overhaul. They have to be familiar with all types of engine.

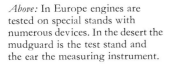

Above: In Europe engines are tested on special stands with numerous devices. In the desert the mudguard is the test stand and the ear the measuring instrument.

Above right: The small Porsche People's Car has rendered the best service in the desert: a few movements suffice to take it to pieces and engine changes take a matter of minutes.

Below right: Breakfast: under cover of canvas to protect against the sun.

Below: Pay day: but as it is impossible to buy anything in the desert the soldiers will become involuntary savers.

Right: Broken springs are common in the desert but mechanics have numerous reserves enabling them to carry out any repair at a moment's notice.

Wings over 'The Blue'

The Afrika Korps were supported in many of their operations in the desert ('The Blue' as it was called by the British) by the Luftwaffe. The Germans were of course the first to perfect the combined use of air and ground forces in their blitzkreig tactics. In the desert the Junkers Ju87 dive-bomber was used extensively against pinpoint enemy positions, whilst Messerschmitt Me109s and Me110s carried out ground strafing roles. This short section illustrates some of the men and aircraft of the Luftwaffe who fought in North Africa. Field Marshal Rommel recognised the vital importance of air support, he said: 'A second essential condition for an army to be able to stand in battle is parity or at least something approaching parity in the air'*. Writing after the defeat of Alam Halfa he warned of the increasing Allied air superiority, inferring that the superior strength of the Anglo-American Air Force was in his opinion going to be the deciding factor in all the battles to come. He also set great store on air supply in desert conditions.

The Rommel Papers Ed Liddell Hart.

With the Stukas at Tobruk

The Junkers Ju87 dive-bomber – the famous Stuka (a name derived from *Sturkampfflug-zeug*) – scored many spectacular successes during the opening blitzkrieg campaigns of the war. Enemy troops were thoroughly demoralised by its screaming dive, as the Stuka blasted ground targets with pin-point accuracy. Provided they had adequate fighter cover, the dive-bombers were extremely effective and were able to deal with a variety of targets in North Africa with equal accuracy, using their steep dive attack. Crews were expected to be able to get at least 50 per cent of their bombs within 25 metres of the centre of the target. The dive from 15,000 feet to the normal release altitude of 3,000 feet took about half a minute and was performed at angles between 60 and 80 degrees. The Ju87B had an automatic device fitted (almost an autopilot) which ensured proper pull-out from the steep dive, because experience in Spain had shown that pilots could black out and lose control.

Here is an account of a series of Stuka bombing raids in and around Tobruk, which

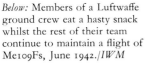

Below: Members of a Luftwaffe ground crew eat a hasty snack whilst the rest of their team continue to maintain a flight of Me109Fs, June 1942./*IWM*

Left: Achtung Stukas! Junkers Ju87-B2 dive-bombers on their way to attack British tanks at Ghobi, 23 November 1941./*IWM*

Below: Camouflage. The value of disruptive camouflage can be seen very clearly in this photograph of a Me109F flying over the desert. The underside was, of course, painted blue to blend with the sky./*Col T. Bock*

is taken from *Balkankreuz über Wüstensand*, published in Germany early in 1943, and kindly supplied to me by the late Colonel Ted Bock.

'On a sultry African morning we sit by our beds. Three visitors have turned up from the desert. They are Arabs – Arabs with turbans, with long flowing beards, and tanned faces. Lean and parched they stand before us, examining us and our machines with their observant, darting eyes.

'Suddenly there's movement on the airfield and we forget all about the three Arabs. In a moment we have fallen in and the *Staffelkapitän* is telling us, "We're involved with land operations today. Our job is to attack an artillery position in the front line in front of Tobruk. This battery has been giving our soldiers a bit of a bad time."

'As we stand by our aircraft, we're told that we'll have to wait a while before take off so we seek protection on our planes from a breeze that has sprung up, and look up at the white clouds, hurrying eastwards. They're going over the same area of sky that we'll soon be crossing. We'll be flying with the clouds, and our path is pointed out for us in red, white and blue – white for the clouds, red for the sand, and blue for the sky and the sea, and the yellow-gold sun stands high above everything.

'It's past midday when the order to start finally comes. We take off amidst clouds of fiery red dust, flight after flight; Stukas, Stukas and yet more Stukas. With us, as fighter protection, Me110s and the Macchis and Fiats of our Italian comrades in arms. When we've all grouped together, high above the field, a thick red bank of dust cloud lies beneath us, thrown up by our take

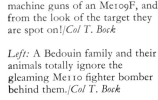

Above: Testing and adjusting the machine guns of an Me109F, and from the look of the target they are spot on!/*Col T. Bock*

Left: A Bedouin family and their animals totally ignore the gleaming Me110 fighter bomber behind them./*Col T. Bock*

Left: The crew of an Me110 on standby. Note the film camera – presumably this was to be a photo-recce mission./*Col T. Bock*

off. Today wind and cloud are our allies. We push on quickly eastwards, at a great height, now over, now under, now in the middle of the white haze. With us over this sea of cloud are our comrades – there "Marie", there "Caesar", over there "Toni", and our neighbouring *Staffel* closes up.

'Now there's no more time left to spend on sightseeing; now everything is serious and dangerous. We attack in two minutes. We race through the cloud cover, break out of the white sea of cotton wool, and there in front of us we can see the ground – hills, roads, tents, forts, artillery positions ... and flak. Fire and smoke spring up from beneath us. Anti-aircraft fire arches white and black around us; beneath us a latticework of red filaments of light. Our flight is tightly grouped. We dive, dive in a wild dance, a whirlwind, a frenzy of movement; we dive into white clouds and red dust, throw ourselves into the black trails of smoke, into the face of lurid fire and strident explosions.

'We dive on the artillery position. We let go our bombs. We pull up ... and fly off. More and yet more Stukas dive from the clouds and drop their bombs. Dust and mushrooms of dense smoke spring up repeatedly from the ground. Have minutes or hours gone past? The harbour looms up ahead of us, with the wrecks of big ships askew across its surface. Now they fall back, disappear under us.

'We regroup while still over English positions. One of our planes is absent from the formation. We have hardly landed however before we hear that it fell behind our own lines – so none of us is missing.

'Once more we crouch by our aircraft and wait to go. Scouts are out, because it has been assumed, with good reason, that English ships have arrived in Tobruk harbour.

'Tobruk is a stronghold ringed so tightly by our besieging forces on land that it can only be supplied by sea. We have good intelligence about how these supplies are carried. More and more the English command is having to use its precious warships to provision Tobruk, for on the one hand there is a shortage of freighters, and on the other the fact that a warship can naturally protect itself better against aerial attack than a merchant ship. However no enemy ship can enter Tobruk in daylight, so they anchor, with heavy fighter protection from the airfields of Alexandria, somewhere off Mersa Matruh and Sidi Barrani. The destroyers, headed for Tobruk are heavily defended with AA weapons.

'The reconaissance flight is back. A cruiser is lying in Tobruk harbour. We fly right behind the commander. Messerschmitts circle us as protection against the English Hurricanes. Because we're diving straight out of the clouds, the Tobruk AA screen sights us

Left: An Me110 having one of its engines changed. Maintenance was extremely difficult in these dusty, sandy conditions at temperatures of over 50° Centigrade./*Col T. Bock*

Below left: Keeping the score. /*Bundesarchiv, Koblenz*

Right: Air raid on Alexandria. Searchlights and flak provide an impressive free firework display over Alexandria. /*Capt A. G. Emery*

Below: Refuelling a flying boat – a Do24T – could be a tricky job even on a calm day. /*Bundesarchiv, Koblenz*

very late. We reach our target almost un-disturbed . . . we dive.

'In front of us the three planes of the *Stabskette* fling themselves down. We roll into a dive, rush vertically downwards. Ever quicker the harbour comes towards us. It's difficult to find our target. They say that somewhere amongst the many wrecks that lie sometimes wholly, sometimes partially in the water, a cruiser has been spotted.

'The wrecks and the harbour grow ever closer. As always, for a moment, we lose the feeling of up and down, of vertical and horizontal. Are we standing still, and is it the earth that is speeding towards us? Is the dark water beneath us rising like a flood towards us? There's the cruiser! There it is! But before we can drop our bombs, great circles of foam like vast craters boil up amidships of the cruiser.

"Bullseye!", shouts the pilot. But we haven't bombed yet. The Leica in my hand weighs a ton. Huge forces press us into our seats. Then it's over. We haven't dropped

Above left: Generalfeldmarschall Albrecht von Kesselring arriving for a visit to the DAK. He was one of the most able of Hitler's generals and took a major part in nearly every campaign in Europe. Originally an artilleryman, he transferred to the air force. As C in C in the south he shared the direction of Rommel's North African campaign.
/Bundesarchiv Koblenz

Left: General Albert Kesselring, photographed during a visit to North Africa./*Col T. Bock*

Above: Reinforcements and supplies going on board a four engined Blomm and Voss flying boat./*Col T. Bock*

Right: Rommel discusses air and ground operations with Generalmajor Frölich who commanded the Luftwaffe elements in support of the DAK. /*Col T. Bock*

Above right: A captured Savoia-Marchetti SM79 *Sparviero* (Hawk) on show in Alexandria. This Italian medium bomber was a highly efficient aeroplane, rated by many as the best land-based torpedo-bomber of the war. It had a crew of four, a maximum speed of 270mph at 12,000ft, a normal range of 1,243 miles and a service ceiling of 22,966ft. In front of the smart Egyptian guard is a 20mm Breda cannon which was used by Italian LAA units./*H. Auger*

Right: British Tommies inspect a crashed German fighter, a Messerschmitt 109, with its distinctive blunt-end wings, some 4½ feet shorter in wingspan than the British Spitfire./*H. Auger*

Below: British soldiers pose beside a captured Italian Fiat CR42 Falco (Falcon). It was the last biplane to be used by any combatant during the war. /*Lt-Col de Salis*

our bombs, it would have been a waste of time. The cruiser is already destroyed. But there – over there on the quay a large warehouse.

Dive!

Bombs away!

'The warehouse is no longer a warehouse but a black mushroom of smoke, in which fire flickers. Only now does it become apparent that the flak is firing, for as we level out, the plane is tossed from side to side. We call it the "Flak dance".

'The second dive has taken us very low and machine guns fire from every nook and cranny. White trails spurt from under our left wing. It smells of petrol. "Hit in left tank", I shout forward.

"We've got enough in the right to get home", he replies.

'The *Staffel* reforms over the sea, and we return to the landing field safely.

"A heavy cruiser, a light cruiser and a tanker sighted on a westerly course to Tobruk, grid reference X-Y". A German reconaissance pilot gives us this information. We are ordered to attack the ships.

'Nothing can show the position of Tobruk more clearly than this terse announcement. The enemy can bring almost anything into Tobruk by cruiser, but not oil or drinking water – a tanker is needed for that. And in order to protect a single tanker, the enemy must call upon two warships. The possession of Tobruk forces the enemy to compromise precious war materials. We fly out over the sea in a north-westerly direction. It's a clear day. The sea beneath us is millpond calm. Only a few sparse clouds accompany us.

Obviously we search the area of sea denoted grid reference X-Y with excited eyes. There's the convoy!

'Even at this great distance the cruisers begin firing. As we close on the ships, prepare to attack, soon will attack, everything goes so uncannily quickly that there's only time for the instinctive combat reaction, and all, all of our attention belongs to the fighting instincts needed for the sortie. No time is left over for the human being, who must stand aside.

'We throw ourselves at the convoy. The heavy cruiser defends itself with its eight AA guns, firing everything at us. But not for long, for two bombs explode on her decks. They blow up right next to the side of the ship, and others rip the sea into huge house-high white fountains. Everything happens in seconds. In seconds we see the small cruiser enveloped in a huge cloud of dense smoke. There, where the quarterdeck must be, the cloud of smoke is at its thickest, and all at once it is lit up redly from within.

'And the tanker? The tanker is still safe and from its decks the crew try desperately to stop the Stukas from attacking by firing machine guns. Where is the tanker? Suddenly we can't see her, only a thick cloud of smoke, from which greedy and angry red arrows of flame jump up into the sky, stationary on the surface.

'In the evening as we sit again by our planes, a scout returns. He says that a large oil slick shown where we have sent the tanker to the bottom. He says that the small cruiser must have shared a similar fate, for only the heavy cruiser, alone and badly damaged, has limped away.'

Below: A crashed Bristol Blenheim aircraft, brought down by AA fire. The Blenheim was one of the RAF's latest light bombers when war broke out./*Col T. Bock*

The Tide Turns

Above: Rommel's new opponent. An informal snap of General Montgomery whose hard fought victory at El Alamein was to prove the turning point in North Africa./*Maj C. Milner*

Right: By day the artillery bombardment continued unabated./*Brig P. A. L. Vaux*

The Beginning of the End

By October 1942 it must have been obvious to someone who was as much of a realist as was Field Marshal Rommel that, unless a miracle occurred, the good days of the DAK were numbered in North Africa. Despite many promises from his superiors he had still not received the extra troops, vehicles and equipment which he so desperately needed. A comparison in mid-October 1942 of tank strengths on both sides showed a 5 to 1 superiority in favour of the Allies, if one discounts the 300 old Italian tanks, the majority of which were so decrepit that they were virtually unfit for action. When one also appreciates that nearly half of the British tanks were reasonably newly-acquired American built Grants and Shermans, whilst only about one sixth of the German tanks were the powerful Pz Kw IV, then the imbalance is even more pronounced. Spielberger & Feist list the opposing tank forces on 23 October 1942 in their book *Armor in the Western Desert* as follows:

British		German	
170	Grants	85	Pz Kw III L/42
252	Shermans	88	Pz Kw III L/60
216	Crusaders 1 & 2	8	Pz Kw IV L/24
78	Crusaders	30	Pz Kw IV L/43
119	Stuarts		
194	Valentines		
1,029		211	

Infantry strengths were, however, more balanced and of course the Germans had constructed a formidable defensive position some eight kilometres in depth, with over five million mines planted in 'Rommel's Devil's Gardens' as they were ominously called. On the debit side also one must not forget the almost never ending lines of communication stretching behind the Afika Korps back to their far off bases, whilst the Eighth Army had a mere 40 miles of easy motoring back to the Delta.

Left: Hour after hour the 25 pounders hurled their shells into the Afrika Korps positions, stabbing the darkness with endless flashes from one end of the El Alamein line to the other. /IWM

Operation Lightfoot

On 23 October 1942, General Montgomery launched Operation Lightfoot, the start of the second and most famous battle at El Alamein, which was to prove the major turning point of the war in North Africa. A massive artillery barrage was followed by powerful attacks in both the north and the south. However, the main weight of these initial thrusts was in the north, the southern attack getting bogged down in the extensive minefields which I have already mentioned. 104 Panzer Grenadier Regiment, as part of 21 Panzer Division, was located in the south next to the Italian Ariete Division. It suffered heavy losses during the Lightfoot operations, especially when switched north to attack the Kidney Ridge salient on 27 October, almost dislodging the British positions there. Typical of the stubborn, bloody fighting during Lightfoot is the story which follows, told by Ralph Ringler, who was then commanding the 10th Company of Regiment 104. His company was ordered on 23 October to guard the eastern end of a safe lane through the minefield belt. His description of the

British barrage is so real that one can almost here the shells exploding and feel the shock-waves as the British guns went on and on remorselessly pounding away.

'Towards dusk we went to the battalion command post, to celebrate the birthday of our commander. We hadn't celebrated in the Desert before, so we were pretty happy. The Adjutant and his staff had put up a very large tent inside which, with much care, a banquet had been prepared – with nothing and out of nothing – and a happy atmosphere prevailed. We stood at the entrance as if we ourselves were being fêted. Then it all became quickly informal; the commander could unfortunately hear little, his ear drums had gone, but his thanks were most cordial. Gefreiter (Lance-Corporal) Kaspar played the harmonica, whilst Unteroffizier (Sergeant-Major) Monier sang folk songs and all present joined in. Alcohol raised our spirits. In the desert only a little wine was needed to warm the heart. Perhaps for many it was their last happy evening. Outside it was peaceful – too peaceful. I kept on thinking about cats and mice. It was late when we weaved our befuddled

way back to our foxholes. Unteroffizier Monier told me for the umpteenth time about his wife and children at home in the Palatinate; he proudly showed me their photograph. "If I could see them once more at home, Lieutenant, just once more". I was helpless in the face of this confidence by the father of a family. I struggled to show understanding but couldn't really understand. "Perhaps later after victory Monier – you'll see them and we'll have all this behind us". This answer seemed futile as I stuck out my hand to him in farewell.

'The "Inferno" came with a bang – with an inhuman relentless series of explosions. The whole desert horizon seemed to burn and to shudder. As I surfaced from a deep sleep, the shock raced through my limbs – the bang was like a battering ram, no, it was the Moloch, the superhuman enemy. It drummed, the explosions were so frequent that one couldn't distinguish them singly. The shells howled overhead and exploded, the ground rocked and the detonations shook me into confusion. I felt a shiver going up my spine. Tommy must have battery after battery up there. No one knew what was up. We could only hope and wait in our miserable foxholes, out of contact with our battalion headquarters.

'A nauseous, slimy morning crept up. In the sky there stood a black-brown smokescreen, the sweet suffocating vapour of gunpowder that hung stubbornly at a uniform height about the ground. The acrid smell mounted horribly in the nose, the heavy pressure pressed on every ear and lung, so the rising sun cheered us up. Rumours grew – finally a message from the staff – in the northern fighting Tommy had partially broken through – a counter-attack was in progress. In the south the attack by the English had been blocked. Plan C was to come into operation calling for increased alertness. My God – as if we didn't know that already! Plan C also meant the regrouping of my position. The manoeuvre was carried quickly as everyone knew what to do. We could at last hope to see the English in front of us – because lying there defenceless, waiting for a direct hit, is really depressing, although up until now we had had no casualties.

'The day was endless, I crawled from strongpoint to strongpoint. Everywhere pallid, worn-out faces; everywhere anxious questions that I couldn't answer. I tried to get provisions for the company. Finally, after hours, a food carrier arrived with a piece of canvas full of hermatically sealed packets of "Afrika bread". It was a disgrace –

for over 100 men there were only 20 tubes of cheese for the whole day; and 10 field bottles of unpalatable "Negrosweat" (cold coffee). To stop their minds from wandering I ordered the weapons to be cleaned – we would need them at some stage.

'I kept on thinking about Unteroffizier Monier, "Will I get home again?" he had asked. And I had to answer that!

'It was half an hour before dusk when a runner fell into my foxhole, "Lieutenant Ringler, to the commander immediately". As a precaution I sent the drivers back to their vehicles, dug in about two kilometres behind the dunes, and got the lads to pack and get ready for movement. Rittmeister (Captain) Mitros had taken over the battalion – Major Ehle headed the regiment. The Rittmeister was very serious, I got into the strongpoint which was covered by a truck chassis. He hardly looked at me and talked crisply and factually. "10 Company is to go through the minefield and occupy Point 115 in 'no man's land'. It is to be built up as a strongpoint and is to be held". He pointed it out on the map. "Here we are three kilometres from the minefield which is about eight kilometres wide. Here is Point 115 at the exit of the minefield right in front of Tommy. The passageway through the field is marked, as far as we know, by the iron poles. Further over there should be an observation post with an assault gun. It reported in about an hour ago – any questions?"

'There were thousands I wanted to ask – but only "No, Herr Rittmeister", came out. "Do it well Ringler, much depends on holding Point 115 – goodbye". I hurried back to the company strongpoint. Finally something to do.

Above: Confident young reinforcements for the DAK move up to the Alamein front by train, October 1942./*IWM*

Left: The DAK artillery replies. A 105mm howitzer belonging to Artillerie Regiment 190 in action at El Alamein./*W. Susek*

Above right: A windswept bivouac just behind the front line positions./*German Armour School*

Right: An AA MG position protecting the guns of Artillerie Regiment 190. /*W. Susek*

'It was dark before I could get the company into their vehicles – 15 of them in all – with two 5cm anti-tank guns. Some of the people had to stay behind. It began to rain – the night was pitch black.

'My greatest worry – would I find the path through the minefield, and if not how do I get through it? The drivers were told to keep the maximum distance possible between vehicles and under no circumstances to leave the column. I drove in the first car – the nearer we got to the minefield the slower I let the driver go. Finally, I saw a few poles on the horizon looking like shell blasted trees. I stopped, got out and was annoyed to find that the other vehicles didn't stop at the correct intervals, so I ran back along the column, made them open out and called the drivers to me. To find the lane I sent two men to the right – Unteroffizier Monier and I went to the left.

'Will it be easily seen? Will it be the right lane? We'd been walking around for a quarter of an hour, our uniforms wet through by the rain, we felt very irritated. Over there, two posts at five metres apart, that must be the

Right: A Pz Kw IV, armed with a long barreled 75mm gun, sits in its sand bagged emplacement, waiting for the British onslaught./*Col T. Bock*

Below: A captured 88mm plus Sd Kfz 7 tower./*IWM*

Right: This *Maschinengewehr* 34 on an AA mounting surrounded by a well constructed stone sangar, was set up to protect the artillery gun position of 190 Artillerie Regiment./*W. Susek*

Below: Battery fire position at El Alamein. A gunlayer at work laying his 10.5cm *leichte Feldhaubitze* 18./*W. Susek*

Bottom: A gun crew pose beside their 10.5cm howitzer in position in the El Alamein area./*W. Susek*

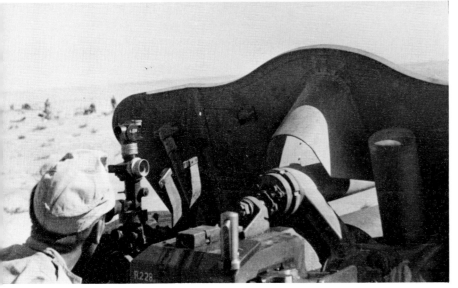

lane – I ran further along it and saw two more posts. Very laboriously we found our way back to the column – the stars had disappeared and carelessly we hadn't noted our route. We mounted and travelled slowly from post to post. The column mustn't get separated – I sat on the radiator of my vehicle – Monier sat on the gun carriage of the first anti-tank gun behind me. There was no fear – only terrific tension. I concentrated totally on not letting the column stray into the minefield. Always ready to react at once, always intent on seeing the next post at the right time. If one watched carefully old vehicle tracks could be seen but the sand had covered them over for the most part. Frequently I had to stop, and go ahead on foot to find the right way.

'Just as we set off again there was a howling noise and a series of shells fell into the minefield lane. Quite close – then a salvo every 30 seconds. A few vehicles wanted to break out, but my NCOs knew their stuff. They knew that only by sticking together could we save the column. Trusting only my instinct and my lucky star, I fumbled along on the right and probable way out. Suddenly my car stopped, I looked at the driver – unsteadily Obergefreiter Miller sobbed "I can't go on". Now this! The column had already started off. Damn it, if a lucky shot ... I pushed Miller to the side, "No, no, no" he stammered. "Let's get out ..." Finally I came down on clutch and gear lever at the same time. Meantime it had begun to rain again – even here – visibility down to nil. Then a shell landed between the vehicles, I

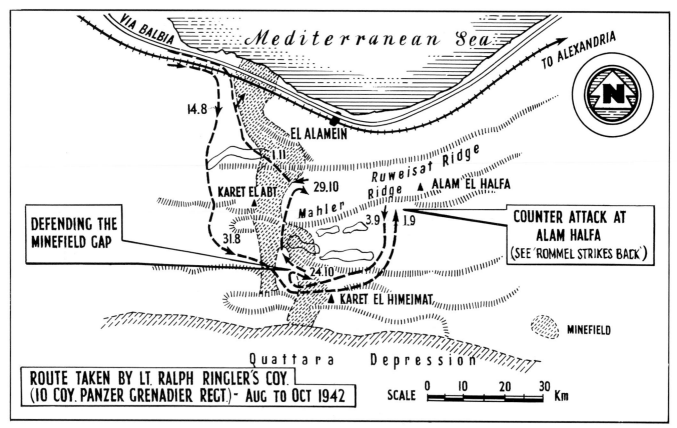

VIA BALBIA

Mediterranean Sea

TO ALEXANDRIA

N

14.8

EL ALAMEIN

Ruweisat Ridge

29.10

KARET EL ABT

Ridge ▲ ALAM EL HALFA

Mahler

3.9 ↕ 1.9

DEFENDING THE
MINEFIELD GAP

COUNTER ATTACK AT
ALAM HALFA
(SEE 'ROMMEL STRIKES BACK')

31.8

24.10

▲ KARET EL HIMEIMAT

MINEFIELD

Quattara Depression

ROUTE TAKEN BY LT. RALPH RINGLER'S COY.
(10 COY. PANZER GRENADIER REGT.) - AUG TO OCT 1942

SCALE 0 10 20 30 Km

stopped and ran back. A truck was slewed diagonally across the track, and the driver was holding his arm. Carefully I directed the other vehicles past it, and breathed again when no one hit a mine. We must have been driving for hours, the English were still shelling the lane through the minefield. Had they seen us or heard us? It made no difference we had to go on. Next to me my driver raved and sobbed – My God – what was I going to do with him? I elbowed him in the ribs.

'Another shell whistled close nearby. Miller screamed like an animal, a terrible shock tore the wheel from my hands and threw the car forward. I trod down hard on the brakes. It hit directly behind me – Monier! I ran back, the vehicle carrying the anti-tank gun was undamaged, the driver lay near the lorry unhurt. "What happened", I called to him, "Where is Unteroffizier Monier?". I suspected something had happened to him. A moan came from a dark patch near the marker poles of the minefield. "Monier, are you all right?" "I knew it would happen", he whispered faintly, "Please my wife . . ." Monier was dead. As if in a trance we started off again. Immediately in front a colossus appears in the night, a tank! The barrel pointed right at me at close range – English?

'I stopped, ran over and signalled like mad the password – "Naples" – "Vesuvius" came back. Point 115 had been reached. The darkness was oppressive, the shelling had slowly ceased. Lieutenant Bauer and his assault gun was nearby in their forward observation post. Without beating about the bush he filled me in. Here we were at the end of the minefield, in front of us to the east – the English. There should also be a screen of Italian tanks in front of us – "Screen of tanks" – such pretty words! We were on a forward slope and there was also an old Italian position on the slope about 300 metres long. "Good luck", and off went Lt Bauer from Vienna.

'For me there now began the most important part of my undertaking, the ordering and securing of the position. We were 98 men to unload the weapons and equipment and to unlimber the two principal items – the anti-tank guns. The vehicles would then be sent back through the minefield, the fresh tracks would lead them and I hoped that Oberfeldwebel (Regimental Sergeant Major) Wigl would get them through to the west side of the minefield where they would wait for us.

'Meanwhile I tried to find the so-called Italian position. Finally I discovered it, half filled-in trenches and foxholes, often only small depressions less than 50 centimetres deep. Here and there an Italian steel helmet, here and there a sandbag. Only hints, but better than nothing. Time was already going too quickly.

'It was one o'clock and raining cats and dogs. The laborious unlimbering of the heavy weapons began. Not many. Two 5cm anti-

Above: Wire, coupled with the minefields, helped to make the German positions extremely difficult to assault. */Bundesarchiv, Koblenz*

tank guns, three heavy machine guns, one grenade thrower – a pitifully small number.

'What we did badly now couldn't be made good by day, so in consultation with my section leaders I was most careful in siting the position of each heavy weapon, the position of each sentry post, the delineation of each section and group. Frequently I went down the slope to make sure of every detail, even in the dark. The anti-tank guns were put in place with great effort, the gunners wheezed and puffed heavily, everybody helped. Finally I could set up my company HQ, it was a depression only a few centimetres deep surrounded by sandbags. In the middle there were more sandbags making two beds. In each two people could lie down next to one another. In one myself and a runner, Gefreiter Fuchs. Unteroffizier Feuerkogel, the company medic, and a second runner occupied the other. Once again I looked over the whole position, in the east it was getting light and there was still so much to do. Food and ammunition had to be given out, boards had to be laid over the trenches and foxholes as protection against the sun. Fatigue numbed my whole body, I had to rest for a while. I blinked in the direction of the English – but I had to sleep, tiredness lay on my head like an iron ring. Was it seconds or hours later when I got up? It could only have been a few minutes, because the sun hadn't crawled right up over the horizon. A salvo of shells fell, at the most 50 metres behind the position, eight explo-

sions, hard and pitiless. A magnificent, an inhuman day dawned, within two minutes the guns had zeroed in onto our position. The monotony of the automatic explosions was nerve racking, as, inactive and helpless, we lay there pressed down into this position. I tried to make out the guns with binoculars so as at least to know from where this torment came, however, it was impossible to make anything out against the sun. Tommy must have seen us immediately it was light, must have noticed that the entrance to the safe lane through the minefield was occupied. Unwillingly I thought of the glorious Italian screen of tanks, if anybody had hit them then they must have been easily ripped apart.

'That was the worst thing, an invisible enemy pinning us down. He could aim each shot unhindered and only needed to correct it after each salvo. It got on your nerves – at some stage it would get you – perhaps the next one or the one after next. I simply couldn't take any more of this inactive lying around. Between two explosions I slithered over to Number Two section, there, in a large hole lay the section leader who was also the anti-tank gun commander. When I crawled under the tarpaulin the people blinked up at me apathetically, then I noticed a small look of satisfaction on their features – there was still somebody who worried about them. "What are we going to do Lieutenant?", they asked.

"Watch out that the tanks don't come too

near to us". That was the only help I could give. "Sleep alternately, but a watch must be kept on the perimeter". Unteroffizier Hanke was the gunlayer, he was from Lower Saxony and taciturn. He looked pleased, however, when I praised him for building up his position so well.

'Now for Number One section and then on to the machine guns. I waited for another salvo and ran to the company HQ in the middle; I heard the whistle of a shell dangerously close – right in the middle of the position – a fountain of sand and stones fell down on me, I pressed myself right into the sand. Then I heard shouts, my God just where I'd been. The tarpaulin was ripped, the sand red, I ran back. Four men had been badly wounded. Hanke was dead – a splinter in his head. Unteroffizier Feuerkogel looked after the wounded. He hadn't attracted my attention until now. He came from the Rhine area but was somewhat the melancholic type, he had done his job up to now quietly and without fuss. Small, dark haired and squat he was the typical right hand man, the sort of person who was there when you needed him and who was around when things got hot. Now he was here. We could only bind up their wounds in a makeshift manner, a tourniquet was applied to Mahnke's arm – we couldn't do much else for him. Once again the tarpaulin was stretched over the position. Lightning never strikes twice says the proverb and therefore we made that area and the depressions nearby a collecting point for the wounded. Hardly had Feuerkogel finished here than Number One section was hit. A couple of men crawled past me with blood streaming from their wounds. In a lull between firing I went over. I myself had had enough, I was determined to devote my final reserve of willpower to finding out where this opponent was who was thoroughly smashing us to pieces, without us being able to do anything in return.

'The violet-yellow of the morning had become a satiated browny-yellow, the sun burnt down remorselessly until I thought that even a direct hit on my foxhole wouldn't make me angry.

'How did my orders read? Hold the position – yes, but against whom? Here we were being slaughtered and run down. If Tommy continued for a few more hours we would all be no more than physical and mental wrecks, it was really hopeless. . . . Suddenly I discovered something; because of the changed position of the sun we could now see in front of us the discharge of the enemy guns from behind a dune. Comically that was very reassuring, as it was no longer merely a noise but now one could see in front the flash and cloud of smoke and there was a heartbeat between firing and the shell landing. I passed on the position of the guns from man to man. Almost immediately I felt an improvement in morale. The ghastly uncertainty no longer weighed so heavily on us now, now I knew that Tommy and his tanks wouldn't have such an easy task. Until now only he could see us – now we could see him as well, what a simple thing but what a comfort.

'I began to make plans; if we could hold on until dark then I would send a runner back to the battalion. At the moment it would mean certain death. If we could only last out then they could send us food and drink, if we could only hold out perhaps we could send the wounded back as well, if we . . .

'But Mahnke's ripped arm – he needed immediate attention – he needed it now, but how? At the moment he was unconscious most of the time. Feuerkogel crawled up to me and reported, things were bad – already almost a third of the company were casualties. Three men had sunstroke and a high fever, the rest were apathetic and physically debilitated. While the medic told me about the casualties I didn't let the malicious dunes opposite us out of my sight. The two minute respite was up again – yes, there was the flash, I felt it coming and dragged Fuerkogel onto the ground behind the miserable wall of sandbags. A short, sharp bang – no, I was still alive and crawled out from a pile of rubble, even our last weak protection had been blown to blazes.

"Feuerkogel what is – Feuerkogel?"

"I've bought it, Lieutenant".

"Rubbish – where?"

'Blood flowed out of his neck, my God, our medic himself wounded and I knew practically no first aid. I dug a bandage from the sand and wrapped it round his neck. The splinter might not be deep and might not be fatal. What happened next was unkind, Tommy had cut short the two minutes pause for breath, instinct told me that this time they were in earnest. With a few strides I was next to the anti-tank gun.

"Where is Feldwebel Fiedler?". How unnecessarily does one create worries for oneself. Fiedler crouched there, almost pressed to the gun looking tensely towards the enemy.

"Lieutenant, they're just coming. I saw movement behind the dunes".

"Fiedler, where are your gunners?"

"I've only got one left".

"Right hurry, Fiedler you're gunlayer. I'll load and Knapp can hand us the ammunition. OK, let's go".

"Here they come!"

'The good Fiedler was now excited and me not a little less. There they came, at perhaps two thousand metres, two, three, four, five, six – no more – seven or eight tanks. They formed up in formation in a wedge in front of the dunes. My heart beat faster – did they realise how few we were? Did they know that the second anti-tank couldn't fire, because the whole gun crew had been wounded and the gunsight had been destroyed?

"Let them come on, Fiedler. That's our only chance. At four hundred metres or closer – and not before, we open fire".

'They were already only a thousand metres away. The artillery guns had stopped firing. I flushed hot and cold at the same time; sweat beaded on my brow. Hadn't Lt Bauer told me last night about the Italians in front of us?

'My God, what if they were Italians?

'At seven or eight hundred metres I tried to make out the type of tank; it was almost impossible in the midday heat haze. Fiedler adjusted the sights, he seemed to be sure of his ground. I wasn't and there was no one there I could ask ... They crawled nearer. Were they Italians or Tommies? Idiot, they are Italians! You're shooting at your own men. Wait a moment! What do you mean wait a moment, their guns are pointed at us – now it doesn't matter which side they're on! "Fire!"

We hit one at 400 metres. A jet of flame shot out of it. From the burning wreck crawl soldiers – blackhaired and in short trousers like soldiers on leave. One jumps down at the side of the tank on fire, others run to the next tank. By then we had that one also in our sights. As they clamber onto it we hit it. There was a terrible confusion over there with the Tommies – are they English? They are really so small, just as if they were Italians. In those shocking moments I had terrible doubts.

'Now the second tank was burning and I was quite sure they were English tanks – they were "Bandits". The survivors of the first two "Bandits" were running over to the third. Some writhed on the ground. The other tanks had stopped at a loss what to do. Hardly had this happened, when a couple of armour piercing shells hit the ground near us. Now they were pushing back – and then we hit the third tank.

'But that was it; if they had made out our position through the smoke from our gun, then we'd had it. Already the end tank had begun to fire at our gun.

"Away from the gun Fiedler".

"Shouldn't we use the machine gun, Lieutenant".

'I was shocked at this idea – I saw the wounded and burnt little men over there.

"No", and if it was ten times wrong, "No".

'The enemy fire wasn't accurate. Gradually the rest of the "Bandits" disappeared behind the dunes. In front of us, in the sand, there died a number of English soldiers, agonisingly, thoughtlessly – men like us.

'We were overjoyed at our defensive success. Morale was high again. Much was forgotten. Fiedler still wanted to fire on them.

"Fiedler, I'm afraid we might have knocked out three Italian tanks".

Now it was quiet.

'Suddenly I couldn't believe my eyes. An English jeep came out from behind a dune. I was just about to give the order to fire, when I saw through my field-glasses a Red Cross flag.

"Feuerkogel, quickly, get some sort of flag and wave it. Tommy wants to pick up his dead and wounded".

'There in the middle of the desert, a few metres below sea level, stood a German unteroffizier waving a dirty shirt ... No shots. That was the chance ...

'While Tommy was worrying about his own people, I ran to my wounded. The less badly hurt were quickly gathered together. Mahnke had to be taken to a hospital as quickly as possible or it would be too late for him. Those who could walk would have to carry the badly wounded. In a few minutes the sad column disappeared into the minefield. We were down to 32 men.

'The English waved their flag again and drove off east with their pile of dead and wounded. After a little while I got Feuerkogel, with his white bandage around his arm and his dirty bit of international law, inside our position again. Everything had become very quiet.

'Our opponents left us alone for almost half an hour. Then once more humanity was cut off by inhumanity. After the breathing space the shelling began again as in the hours before.

'Despondency fell over us. This was a great anticlimax after the great tension. Anxious questions still hung in the air – what would the enemy do now? What would we do? One thing was certain ... we couldn't stand another day like this. Our canteens, used so sparingly, held only a few drops of water. Most of us suffered from a raging thirst; many were incapacitated by it. It was now 4pm.

'The whole time I was searching the dunes to our front with the field glasses. Suddenly I was wide awake, concentrating. To the northwest, perhaps two or three thousand metres away, in any case out of range, drove a wedge of tanks without any opposition from our side – direction west. There were about 15 tanks. Perhaps they were the new Shermans? Obviously there was a way through the minefield up there as well. We had to look on helplessly as the English sent them to attack us in the rear.

'In spite of this I wanted to try something. I decided to run to the observation post about 500 metres behind us. Perhaps there I could get in touch with battalion HQ. It was slightly uphill, the assault gun stood just behind the crest of the dune. I'd hardly been running stooped for a few moments when all around me bullets began to sing. At first I didn't pay any attention; only when I saw the sparks of the ricochets, with me, lying in the middle of the stretch of sand as if on a tray; but I had to go on. The chances were same going back or forward. The only consolation was that the machine gun must be quite a long way off. In spite of this the fire became more accurate, but with a last despairing leap I jumped over the dune. I couldn't speak and for minutes thought my chest would burst. I saw Lieutenant Bauer, he seemed pretty tired out as well.

"Congrats on your three 'Bandits'."

"And I thought that they were Italians . . ."

"Nonsense . . . obviously English".

Somehow I felt relieved.

"If they had come on a bit we would have helped – but I can only shoot if the observation post is directly threatened".

"Thanks! Can you let me get in radio contact with the battalion?"

"We can try – perhaps I can go through Division".

'I sent this message: "Situation report – about 15 enemy tanks have broken through approximately 3,000m north. My company reduced to 32 men, one anti-tank gun and one machine gun still working, no food, no water, little ammo, three enemy tanks knocked out. Please send further orders soonest".

'Tommy fired at me on my return journey. Each stride, each leap had me thinking "Kismet, Kismet, Kismet . . . ". Totally blown I fell to the ground, thankful towards my Kismet.

'Slowly the sun went down below the horizon. Still no news from Lieutenant Bauer. He had promised to bring any answer over immediately. Meanwhile the artillery fire had increased. As twilight made the desert violet, observation for the English must have been very difficult – so I sent Gefreiter (Lance Corporal) Kater to the observation post. I watched him run with agitation and only breathed again when he disappeared safely behind the dune ridge. Immediately afterwards he reappeared and excitedly waved his arms. Visibility was really very bad. Extremely alarmed I awaited his return.

"The observation post has received a direct hit", he said, "only the driver of the assault gun is still alive. The radio was destroyed. The Lieutenant was hit in the head by a splinter – nothing could be found of the others".

Above: Afrika Korps soldiers hit the deck as British shells explode in front of them./*Keystone Press*

"Did our report get over?"

"The driver thought that it did".

So we waited.

'The burning tanks a few hundred metres in front of us eerily lit up the darkness. I put together a scouting party of volunteers for reasons of safety – I wanted to know whether there was anything to be found over by the tanks or whether an enemy scout troop wanted to go over to the tanks under cover of darkness. Minutes went by endlessly. Then . . shots.

'I sent out five men – only four came back. Three fell out, shut their eyes and lay panting; one reported:

"We were just about to turn round when something made a noise. We were like targets on a shooting range, silhouetted by the burning tanks and had to get away as quickly as possible. Kranzhuber was hit – dead. We couldn't bring him back with us or we'd all have had it. We shot back and must have hit one of them. We'll still get Kranzhuber, Lieutenant".

'Then in the silence – the screams. At first they could hardly be heard, then they penetrated one's consciousness, became louder, they could no longer be ignored, then they became inhuman, animal.

'Without any orders there were suddenly four men with me. The others wouldn't have been woken by the last trumpet on the Day of Judgement. Quickly we worked our way in from the side to the still glowing and smoking wrecks.

'Gradually the screams died out. The tone was resigned, no longer summoning, only now a man crying – only the noise of a dying

Above: Another concentration of shells falls upon the pock marked desert./*Bundesarchiv, Koblenz*

agonised creature. Then we saw them in front of us. They lay quite close together – Kranzhuber dead, lying on his back. His cap had slipped off his head. He lay there peacefully, his arms folded rectangularly next to his head, like a sleeping child.

'The Englishman had left a broad trail of blood behind him. He had crawled to Kranzhuber and his blood-smeared hands were closer and closer to Kranzhuber's still hands. His life ran from him, his red head looking redder in the glow of the tanks. He had wanted to be with someone at his death – but had only found another corpse.
It was senseless.
Doggedly we dug and hacked away a grave.
Deep and wide.

'Deeper and wider as if it was to protect us also. Carefully we laid them in it together. We put Kranzhuber's weapon in and filled it with sand and stones. The cap and steel helmet we put above. Two more mothers would wait in vain.
It was stupid. A common grave was little compensation.

'Totally exhausted and burnt out I took notice of Feldwebel Fiedler's message. "Orders from the battalion, sir, we're to go through the minefield at once". Nothing else. "Lieutenant, almost all the men are exhausted and asleep, I don't know how to rouse them". There was heavy breathing next to me. Gefreiter Kater and Unteroffizier Feuerkogel were so deeply asleep, that it seemed almost a sin to wake them.

'The desert and the glowing wrecks now had an exciting effect, once more there was an objective – a new spirit woke inside us.

In a few minutes the section and group leaders were with me, that is those who were still here, those unwounded or their deputies. Our withdrawal must be quick and silent, the English mustn't realise that we were leaving the position, at least until it was too late. One group after another would crawl over the edge of the dune and then through the minefield; they would collect at the other end. I sent my driver with the first group so that he could drive in my car to the one-time observation post – we wanted to take the dead with us. The wounded and those who couldn't walk we would carry on the assault gun. I myself and Feldwebel Fiedler would wait until last and after the last group had left we would spike the anti-tank gun that could no longer be transported.

'The awakening and getting up of the men was the worst part, most slept the sleep of the dead. We beat them with clenched fists and after a lot of urging the first ones crawled off. The undamaged anti-tank gun had to be hoisted up the overhang. Without commands. There were only a few men who could even work to some small extent. Breathing heavily and struggling for air we pushed it over the crest of the dunes. More and more fell away and couldn't continue, but finally after twenty minutes exertion we did it. The men fell down behind the dunes as if dead, I had to go back to the position, only one group of six men were there – and the wounded. Suddenly a short whistling and right next to us a shattering explosion – no time to take cover.

'Gunner Lukas cried out and clutched at his foot; Kater stayed down, I crawled over to him, his face was chalk white – dead? A

83

Left: The blinding flash of a direct hit on an enemy AFV makes a graphic picture as this panzer engages the advancing British armour at night. */Bundesarchiv, Koblenz*

Below: Litter of personal kit left behind in the Afrika Korps positions opposite El Alamein. */IWM*

Bottom: Parachutists belonging to the Ramcke Brigade withdrawing through the desert. On 6 November 1942 they managed to hijack a complete British supply column and, after covering 200 enemy infested miles, rejoined Rommel's retreating *Panzerarmee*. */Keystone Press*

pool of blood gathered underneath his cap. Carefully I lifted the cap off, a splinter had torn away the scalp off the back part of his head, but he was still alive. He moaned softly and looked at me with clear eyes.

"Does it hurt Kater?" No answer, only a shaking of the head.

'Had the English noticed our intentions or was it only an aimless barrage? If they decided to attack we few couldn't do anything. So get away, as quickly as possible away.

'We put an explosive charge into the barrel of the second anti-tank gun and carefully watched the perimeter to see that nothing went wrong in the last moments. Then I sent off the last sad procession. They tied Kater onto the outside of the assault gun; Lukas, thank God, had only a flesh wound. We fastened the anti-tank gun behind the assault gun with cords and cable. At last they could go off, hopefully they would get through the minefield all right. I told Fiedler to light the fuse, and then nothing left but to get away. If Tommy hadn't realised anything yet, now it must have slowly dawned on him that we were up to something. It was more than three hours since the first of us went, it must have been midnight or later, but both our watches had stopped. We had lain down behind the ridge of the dunes. Next to us lay the three corpses, Monier, Hanke and Bauer. The moon had turned the desert into a silver shimmering landscape, our torn nerves wouldn't let us go to sleep. The crack of the explosive charge on the anti-tank gun didn't worry us, if Tommy came we couldn't do anything about it, if only the car would

84

come. I was semi-conscious, nothing disturbed the English, perhaps they thought that our ammo had gone up, perhaps they'd send a troop of scouts. I couldn't care less. My God was it too early? I thought I heard the noise of an engine or had only two minutes gone past? I nudged Fiedler, he had heard the noise as well. Were the English advancing? One couldn't tell from which direction the noise was coming, but it was coming nearer. Then we saw my car appearing out of the minefield, the driver's body shook. The journey through the minefield had hit his nerves hard.

"Lieutenant I can't drive back". So I had to drive myself. We carried the corpses on the back, their feet could be seen over the edge of the car. They were motionless and stiff. I covered them with a tarpaulin.

'The moon stood behind us and mechanically I registered that the shadow of the dead feet could be seen right next to me on the sand. Fiedler sat beside me, the driver stood on the running board next to him. I started off slowly, again the agitation not to lose the path through the minefield, even despite the fresh tracks of the assault gun in front of me. Once I thought that I'd lost the path, then another time I was afraid that I'd lost the corpses. Again and again and more and more often I had to look at the shadow of the feet to see if they were all still there. Again and again we went through roughed up sand into which the jeep almost sank fast. In addition I could smell burnt oil – that could only come from the clutch. The cold moon landscape, the smell, the monotonous grinding of the

wheels, the shadows of the feet, on and on without end – how long eight kilometres could be. I was afraid we would never reach fresh air, the smell of the burnt oil tore my nerves even more, the feet – and the shadows; the shadows were the most frightening.

'Were they alive? The shadows were alive, the men were dead. I started – I had fallen asleep. Hours, seconds? "Fiedler, what's that?" Fiedler was asleep next to me, the driver said, "The company – we're through!" Mechanically I stopped, exhausted my hands dropped from the wheel. My head was heavy and thick. Good God you're the leader of these souls. With difficulty I crawled out of the seat and dropped to the ground. Deep breaths, I tried to speak. Nothing, then the next time – the same. I walked around, I couldn't shout any more – only a soundless cawing came from my throat. I couldn't do anything, perhaps I could counteract it here, I tried to do it by thumping – impossible – nothing more than a murmur could be heard.

'The assault gun wasn't there, it had driven on; here there were about 30 men perhaps fewer. I lay down on the hard cold sand to think.

'Morning dawned as I had my first thought, they were six stiff feet, the shadows of the three corpses in the moonlight. My God I certainly wouldn't have lost my dead. Or was everything that lay here dead? In the dawn light I saw my car, I saw the sleeping Fiedler, I saw three stiff figures in the back, I saw a number of dark patches lying motionless and at peace.

Above: Surrender. On 4 November 1942 the Afrika Korps commander, General der Panzertruppe Wilhelm Ritter von Thoma, surrendered to the British at El Alamein. He is seen here saluting Montgomery before dining with him. Some say he deliberately allowed himself to be captured and talked volubly to his captors about Rommel's further plans and troop dispositions./*IWM*

Right: Carrying their wounded, the DAK's retreat begins./*IWM*

Below: German and Italian prisoners of war trudging through the streets of Cairo near the Citadel. In the distance is the Mahomet Ali Mosque./*IWM*

'The noise of motors and three jeeps came out of the desert; with washed, rested and smart drivers.

'I myself drove the car with my three dead back to the old company HQ and then further on to the battalion – I didn't let them out of my sight while I reported to the commander. In spite of this they would stay in the desert forever, they would become the dust and the sand of the desert'.

The Withdrawal Begins

After 12 days of hard fighting the Alamein battle was over and the long withdrawal had begun. I use the term 'withdrawal' advisedly, because in truth at no time during the remaining agonising months, until the fall of Tripoli on 23 January 1943, did the withdrawal become a rout. Fighting doggedly and with great skill the DAK fell back from position to position. The only order which Rommel chose to ignore was Adolf Hitlers', totally unrealistic 'Victory or Death' signal which was so patently idiotic as to prove to the Afrika Korps, if they really required further proof, of their Führer's complete lack of interest or understanding of the true situation in Africa.

A Rearguard Action

Captain Heinz Werner Schmidt, who we met earlier as one of Rommel's personal staff officers, commanded a special all-arms group during the withdrawal. Here is how he described a rearguard action in which his unit took part:

Above: Rommel moving at speed in his Sd Kfz half tracked recce car nicknamed 'Greif' (Strike). /R. *James Bender*

'When the last of the panzers rolled westward, our task began. We were to be Rommel's rearguard. We pulled out last of all, and had retreated only a few miles along the coast road when we were engaged by armoured cars immediately south of the road. Our guns went into action, and we fought them off. The Special Group moved back in leap-frog movements. One battalion was always halted in defensive positions to cover the retreat, and then it would "up guns" and off. We reached Mersa Matruh on 6 November 1942. I was ordered to take up temporary positions in Matruh's southern defence line and on both sides of the Siwa track. I sited anti-tank guns – each of my companies had five or six of them – at the most important tactical points. Our positions lay between the bunkers where the barbed-wire entanglements and minefields had been left intact as they had been in June when Auchinleck's men had thought to hold this line.

'Late that afternoon I sighted British tanks on a rise south of Matruh. As darkness fell they opened fire on my positions along the oasis track. The pursuit was relentless. Under cover of darkness the surviving columns of our Panzer groups left the stronghold and resumed their westward march. A few hours later a despatch-rider brought me a written situation report. From it I learned that Montgomery's spearheads were already west of Matruh. I could expect orders at about midnight to abandon my present rearguard positions. I was to pull out on a given compass bearing, which alone would take me to the sole remaining passage through the minefield. I remember regretting that I would not have a chance of locating and marking the entrance to the minefield gap in daylight; but at any rate it was a relief to know that during the night we should have a chance to evade the enemy, for it was a certainty that we should be trapped if we remained outside Matruh much longer.

'My driver and the despatch-rider blacked out my truck with blankets. By the glow of a little bulb wired off a battery, we swallowed a meal from cans, and wrote letters home. Busy writing, I failed to note that midnight had come and long since gone. The "Phutt! Phutt!" of a motorcycle. The machine stopped, and a voice called out, "Is that Special Group 288?" A hoarse whisper: "Shut up! Tommy can probably hear you!" The despatch-rider was led to me. A hand was thrust through the black-out blankets. A voice repeated the written order. I read: "Matruh evacuated. Rearguard to follow immediately!" By now I had perfected the drill. Each detachment in the battalion had a messenger detailed to wait near my truck. Instructions took a moment or two, and then their vehicles were moving silently through the darkness to the gun positions. The guns were limbered up, ammunition loaded, and from all sides vehicles converged to form up near my vehicle in a slight wadi. But in spite of every care, the noise of running motors could not be muffled entirely, and I was both annoyed and concerned because several

drivers had shouted while making contact with each other.

'My column had just formed up when – "What was that?" Explosions, a crashing and a whizzing around us. Tank shells were plunging into the ground almost at our feet and whistling between trucks. Some vehicles were hit and burst into flame. At once we were lit by a lurid light – a lovely target for the British tanks, which must be hard upon our southern front. I calculated that there were not many of them, but it was now too late – indeed, it would be futile – to dig in. We must pull out as ordered. But in case we had to halt and dig in, I thrust a short entrenching tool through my breast strap and diagonally across my shoulder. This action was almost to cause our undoing.

"At extended intervals – march!" I shouted the order and, standing in my truck, kept my eyes on the compass needle so as to navigate through the darkness to the minefield gap. We drove through a minor storm of enemy shells. The drivers had only one aim – to get out of range of the pursuing tanks, and their convoy discipline faltered. Contrary to orders, the trucks closed in upon each other and sometimes even raced side by side despite the extended-order drill. Gradually the shelling petered out. I was about to draw a sigh of relief when there was a roar and a jolt. My truck lurched to a stop: radiator and engine were smashed.

"Damn! Tanks ahead!" was the thought that flashed through my mind. "The bastards have cut us off". I shouted an order to my driver, who was just slightly wounded. "Jump to it!" Away from here, I thought. Only speed will get us out of this jam. We leaped on the vehicle following ours. "Forward, don't deviate!" I yelled at the driver.

But there was to be no forward dash for that truck. Again that flash, crash and jolt. The driver and two other men in the truck were wounded. Though I was sitting in the cab too, I escaped unscathed. As I leaped from the truck I saw to the right two brilliant flashes, and then heard two explosions. "This is senseless", I thought. Then I shouted: "Dismount! Dig in!"

'The command was almost unnecessary. Every vehicle had halted. Many of the men were already flat on the ground. But – extraordinary, this – there was an immediate dead calm disturbed only by a few purring engines.

'Now and again a desultory shell flew overhead from our rear – a few last cracks at us from the pursuing tanks. But who the devil was firing at us from the front? Only then did the thought strike me: Are we being fired on, or have we run into a minefield? I scarcely needed to take those few strides forward and examine the ground just behind the nearest destroyed truck. Yes, there was the tell-tale hole. Mines! I was puzzled. My reading of the compass had been dead accurate, I was sure, despite the break-neck speed at which we had travelled. But ... a hot prickling crept over my skin: that entrenching tool! Of course, the steel spade had caused a deviation of the compass needle. The night was fairly dark. I held the compass close to my eyes and took a bearing on its palely luminous glimmer. Then I threw the entrenching tool away and took the bearing again. As I had expected, the needle pointed considerably farther to the left. I had been foolish. Here we now were in the middle of a minefield, with enemy tanks hard behind us. It was up to me to retrieve the situation. I wrapped my mind in calmness, made my

plan, and, with the men lying prone, stepped out to look for the edge of the minefield. A soldier who had robbed a comrade, and had in consequence been dishonoured when I called him a *Schweinehund* on a battalion parade a few days before, now insisted on accompanying me. He ran about regardless of danger, examining tracks and casting an eye round for mines.

'Usually, we knew, the lighter and more easily detonated anti-personnel mines were sprinkled liberally round the heavier plate mines employed against panzers and trucks. But it seemed that here the plate mines were smaller than the usual type, and there seemed to be no anti-personnel mines.

'At length I discovered a rusty strand of barbed-wire, which indicated the edge of the minefield, and I soon located the gap. We had missed it by 50 yards. Only the leading vehicles and guns were actually within the minefield. With most of the men deployed in defensive array, I had the drivers of the rear vehicles head towards the gap. Other squads were detailed for the tricky and not entirely pleasant task of man-handling the endangered vehicles and guns backward over their original tracks to the edge of the minefield. One mine exploded, but fortunately it killed no one. The desert all round us was dead quiet. Not a shot was heard. It took two hours to get the column safely into formation again and moving through the passage. I had lost four valuable vehicles, but none of the men was killed. At the western perimeter a squad of anxious sappers were waiting for us. No sooner had we passed than they mined the gap. Half an hour later they overtook us and sped on'. *

*With Rommel in the Desert by H. W. Schmidt.

Above: This 15cm heavy artillery gun (*schwere Feldhaubitze* 18) was knocked out and captured by the British./*Brig P. A. L. Vaux*

Top left: Rommel in 'Greif' watches a battle. Note also the medical Volkswagen and ambulance waiting in the wings to pick up the inevitable casualties. /*R. James Bender/The National Archives*

Bottom left: A tank battle in progress. Shermans move into fire positions close to what looks to be a burning Pz Kpfw III. /*HQ RAC Centre*

The End in Africa

Operation Torch – Enemy to the Rear

Whilst the Afrika Korps was fighting its skilful delaying action through Cyrenaica and Tripolitania, a fresh menace had appeared behind them in the shape of the successful Allied landings on the coast of Algeria and Morocco. Here is how a British war correspondent, Mr A. D. Divine, who was at the time attached to the US Combat Forces, described the initial assault:

'At one o'clock on the morning of 8 November 1942, the greatest armada that has ever assembled fell on three points on the coastline of Northern Africa.

'The politico-strategic problem involved in the French colonial possessions in Africa was of an extraordinary complexity. It is difficult to conceive the vastness of the French North and West African possessions. Almost half the Mediterranean coast of Africa belongs to France; more than half the west coast from Spanish Morocco to the mouth of the Congo belongs to her. The vast hinterland is conjoined; and under the Vichy regime this whole area, except for Equatorial Africa, was potentially hostile. The major problems that faced the Allied chiefs of staff were those of denying North Africa to the enemy, of secur-

ing it with its enormous wealth both of raw materials and strategic positions for ourselves, of cutting off Rommel's rear, and of carrying out the whole operation with the greatest possible economy of shipping and material.

'Dakar had been attempted once before. The new strategy disregarded Dakar. The plan, as it was carried out, provided for the capture of the northern coastline both on the Atlantic and on the Mediterranean, and assumed that, with Morocco, Algeria and Tunisia in Allied hands, French West Africa and the great Sahara regions to the south would fall without bloodshed. To make certain of North Africa it was necessary to hold four main strategic ports: Casablanca to ensure the possession of Morocco with its potential of warlike tribes; Oran (only 525 miles from Marseilles and possible reinforcement) and Algiers (only 850 miles from Naples) to secure the enormous territory of Algeria; Tunis to cut finally Rommel's supply lines and to deny him a short sea route of escape.

'If all four points had been equally easy of access, there would have been no North African campaign. But the last sector of the vast French African coastline lay within

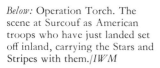

Below: Operation Torch. The scene at Surcouf as American troops who have just landed set off inland, carrying the Stars and Stripes with them./*IWM*

Above: Headed by 'Old Glory' the leading American troops set off for Maison Blanche aerodrome./*IWM*

Right: Operation Torch. More than 20 US Navy landing barges swarm about a mother ship off Safi, French Morocco. Some are leaving for shore whilst others return for new cargoes of men and equipment./*IWM*

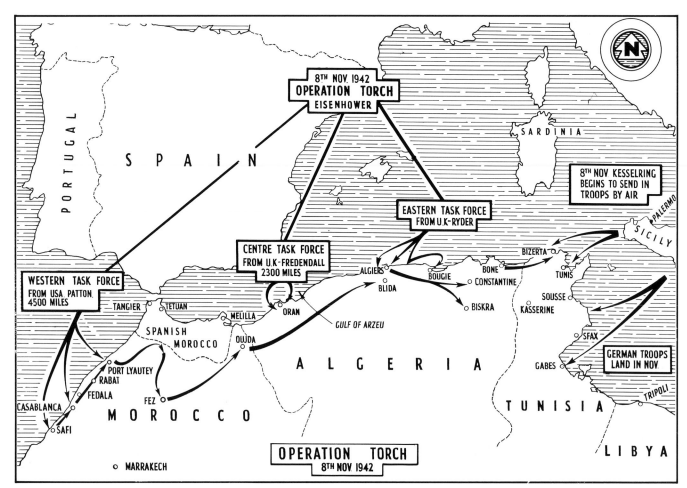

WESTERN TASK FORCE
FROM USA, PATTON,
4500 MILES

8TH NOV. 1942
OPERATION TORCH
EISENHOWER

CENTRE TASK FORCE
FROM U.K-FREDENDALL
2300 MILES

EASTERN TASK FORCE
FROM U.K-RYDER

8TH NOV KESSELRING
BEGINS TO SEND IN
TROOPS BY AIR

GERMAN TROOPS
LAND IN NOV.

OPERATION TORCH
8TH NOV 1942

PORTUGAL
SPAIN
SARDINIA
PALERMO
SICILY

TANGIER
TETUAN
MELILLA
ORAN
GULF OF ARZEU
ALGIERS
BLIDA
BOUGIE
CONSTANTINE
BONE
BIZERTA
TUNIS
SPANISH MOROCCO
OUJDA
BISKRA
SOUSSE
KASSERINE
PORT LYAUTEY
RABAT
FEDALA
FEZ
SFAX
ALGERIA
GABES
CASABLANCA
SAFI
MOROCCO
TUNISIA
TRIPOLI
MARRAKECH
LIBYA

range of the Luftwaffe's Sicilian bases.
The theoretic bomb line cut the African
coast about Algiers: beyond Algiers it
was belived that large-scale operations
would be impossible without large scale
air cover. It was decided, therefore, that
three of the four ports should be invaded
from the sea – Casablanca, Oran and Algiers –
and Tunis should be attacked from the land
as soon as the bases were secure.

'The Vichy Government had declared un-
equivocally that it would resist any attack on
its colonial possessions – a declaration imple-
mented at Dakar, in Syria, in Madagascar.
The Allies, therefore, decided to attempt to
"soften up" that resistance. The landing and
re-embarkation of three British and four
American officers, headed by Major-General
Mark W. Clark (US Army), from a British
submarine, commanded by Lieutenant N. L.
Jewell, on the North Africa coast is among
the more remarkable episodes of the war.
Contact was made by sympathisers; considerable sums of money were expended; and it
was confidentally belived in many quarters
that, in view of the fact that the initial landings were to be made by American troops,
the groundwork done by General Clark and
his party coupled with the traditional friend-
ship between America and France would
suffice to prevent bloodshed. That view dis-

regarded the intransigence of a section of the French authorities in North Africa.

'The organisation of the convoys, their routing through the submarine-infested waters of the Atlantic, their passage through the Straits of Gibraltar and the Mediterranean narrows under the potection of the Royal Navy are among the great masterpieces of naval warfare. They, and the Casablanca convoy sailing from America, arrived off the invasion points *without loss*. Invasions are most vulnerable upon the sea. By zero hour – 1 am on the morning of 8 November – the Allies had won the first round without a blow. The second round – the landing of the forces under Lieutenant-General Dwight Eisenhower, Allied C-in-C North Africa – was different.

'At Algiers, where most of the preparatory work had been done, there was only a token resistance. We lost two destroyers, the *Martin* and the *Broke*, the latter in forcing the boom. Resistance on shore was confined to the area about the Amirauté, to a few sporadic outbursts on the beaches, and to a certain amount of sniping.

'At Oran, with its memories of the attack on the French warships there in 1940 – an attack the absolute necessity of which was underlined in every phase of this brief campaign – resistance was determined. The Oran

assault began with an attempt to seize the salient points in the harbour itself. Two ex-American coastguard cutters, the *Hartland* and the *Walney* which had formed part of the escort of the great convoy of the invasion on the way over, went in without covering fire. At ten minutes past three on the morning of 8 November, HMS *Walney* broke the Oran boom. She was followed by HMS *Hartland* and two MLs. With an almost inconceivable gallantry they pressed home their attack under heavy fire from warships and coastal batteries. Both ships reached their objectives; both ships were sunk with heavy loss of life. For his part in this operation, Acting-Captain F. T. Peters, DSO, DSC, who took the *Walney* into Oran, was awarded the Victoria Cross.

'Meanwhile, east and west of Oran, the American army was getting ashore. At Arzeu Beach, to the east, opposition was overrun swiftly and landing operations began in excellent weather. To the west at X and Y beaches and at Les Andalouses there was no opposition. At once flying columns of armour from the extremities of the landing points swung deep into the country behind in a 70-mile wide pincer movement. The attempt made to capture the aerodrome with parachute troops carried out by the 12th US Air Force (commanded by Brigadier-General James H. Doolittle and flown from England) failed; but

Left: Operation Torch. Transports, silhouetted by the slanting rays of the sun, wait off-shore during landing operations at Mers-El-Kebir in the Oran area of Algeria./*IWM*

Above left: The barn at the Abbaci farm as it is today. The Arab photographed in front of it is one of the two children involved in the incident recounted by Hans Teske./*Hans Teske*

Above: Oberstleutnant Walther Koch, CO of 5 Parachute Regiment, sitting in the car from which he jumped to prevent the execution of the British parachutists./*Hans Teske*

93

brilliant support from British escort carriers smashed the French fighter squadrons at La Senia and at Tafaroui. Though the French fought stubbornly, by nightfall on the Sunday it was clear that Oran could not endure the assault for long.

On Monday vigorous and stiffening resistance at St Cloud, which had been the limit of advance on the Sunday evening, held up the infantry attack from the east under General Allen. On the west Brigadier-General Theodore Roosevelt, commanding the 26th Combat Team, was held on the high ridge of the Djebel Murdjadjo. But behind the battle of the infantry the claws of the armour had closed. The tanks of Combat Command B – the American armoured force under General Oliver – thrusting through St Barbe du Tletat to Tafaroui and up the road to La Senia, were about to link with another section of the same force under Colonel (afterwards Brigadier-General) P. M. Robinnet coming from the western beaches along the northern shore of the great salt lake of the Grand Sebkra. That night Allen's infantry bypassed St Cloud to north and south, and by dawn it was on the last of the heights above Oran. Admirable gunnery from the heavy ships of the Royal Navy was pounding the coastal batteries into submission. In the middle of the morning General Oliver threw his tanks into the city, the infantry came down the last slopes, and the battle was over.

'At Casablanca they still fought. The French ships there put up a vigorous resistance, using submarines, destroyers, and the guns of the great battleship *Jean Bart*. But the

Above: Newly arrived American Sherman tanks line a street in Bizerte, the Allied supply base in Tunisia./*IWM*

Right: This striking night action picture shows British warships firing back at German aircraft which have been attacking shipping in Algiers harbour./*IWM*

Jean Bart was bombed and put out of action, the destroyers were sunk; and at Mehdia, Fedhala and Safi, as well as at Casablanca itself, troops got ashore and the beach heads were secured. The useless fighting went on. But from the very start it was clear that Major-General George S. Patton, in command of the Allied Forces in Morocco, had the situation completely in hand, and on Wednesday, 11 November, all French resistance in North Africa ended by order of Admiral Darlan, Vichy Defence Minister, who happened to be on an inspection tour of French North Africa at the time of the Allied landings. The first phase of the campaign was over. The second was under way'.*

The Axis fights back
The ease with which the Allied landings had been achieved and the apparent lack of enemy reaction did much to foster an air of complacency among the newly arrived American and British forces. Indeed, they must have wondered why Montgomery's Eighth Army

The Second Great War edited by Sir John Hammerton.

had found it such a hard slog to push back an ailing Rommel and his weakened Afrika Korps across Cyrenaica and Libya. It would be simple to clear Tunisia and to hold it as a jumping off place for future attacks onto the continent of Europe. The Allies were soon to have their self confidence severely dented. Kesselring, overall commander of German forces in the Mediterranean area, began pouring reinforcements into Tunisia, until by the end of November, there were already 25,000 German and Italian troops there with 100 tanks, including a heavy tank battalion equipped with Tiger tanks. They were under the command of General der Panzertruppe Walther Nehring, who had commanded the Afrika Korps until he was wounded in the arm in late August 1942. Nehring was ordered back to North Africa in November 1942, the task of 'Stab Nehring' being to plan the establishment of the German bridgehead in Tunisia. Stab Nehring became XC Korps on 19 November and, as the forces were built up, became Pz AOK 5 on 8 December. Gen Nehring handed over command one day later to Generaloberst Jürgen von Arnim, with

Above: Men of the 5th Bersaglieri Regiment in action during the Axis withdrawal. The cock feathers in their helmets make them easily recognisable. They were among the best Italian troops to fight in North Africa. (Reproduced here by kind permission of Stato Maggiore dell 'Esercito).
/Stato Maggiore dell 'Esercito

Above: The Battle of Medenine, 6 March 1943. In order to try to save the Mareth Line and halt Allied progress Rommel launched savage armoured and infantry attacks in the Medinine area. During the battle the 6pdr anti-tank gun, seen in this photograph, was commanded by Sgt Crangles of 1st/7th Queens. He destroyed 10 German tanks, most of which can be seen still smoking in front of the gun position, but was eventually put out of action by a direct hit. The crew then fixed bayonets and prepared to resist to the last, but were overrun by three undamaged enemy tanks. Sgt Crangles was awarded the Distinguished Conduct Medal for his bravery. /*Maj P. N. Erskine*

Right: The Mareth hills. The Eighth Army crossed into Tunisia in early February 1943 and captured Medenine in front of the Mareth line on 16 February. /*Maj C. F. Milner*

Right: Blockhouses in the Mareth line, which the 8th Army reached on 24 February 1943. They fought a series of tough battles before the Afrika Korps withdrew in early April./*Maj C. F. Milner*

Below: Men of the East Yorkshire Regiment 'mopping up' in one of the trench systems of the Mareth line. This was Rommel's last battle in North Africa and he flew home to Germany a few days later./*IWM*

Generalleutenant Ziegler as his deputy. By Christmas the Allied advance had been halted and the race for Tunis lost.

A Parachute Action

Unfortunately space does not allow me to deal with this part of the Tunisian campaign in detail, but there is room for one short, but dramatic, story of an action involving British and German parachutists. The German paras were members of Ramcke's Parachute Brigade which had already done incredible feats in the desert. One of their number, Hans Teske, now living in England, remember the Tunisian incident thus:

'The 2nd Battalion of the British Parachute Regiment had been dropped near Depienne not far from Tunis on 29 November 1942. The actual landing was uneventful, however, there were some casualties. One man was killed when his chute failed to open and there were also some ankle injuries. Lt Buchanan, whose half-platoon had failed to become airborne, was ordered to remain at the DZ to look after the injured while the battalion moved on towards Tunis. Unknown to the British paras, the drop had been observed by German paras manning the German main line of defence nearby. After a short battle, in which one German was killed, Lt Buchanan and his men were forced to surrender. The commander of the joint German/Italian force, Hauptmann Hans Jungwirt, ensured the well-being of the casualties from both sides and arranged for their removal to a hospital. This was followed by a short interrogation of the remaining prisoners. Jungwirt, however, had to leave with his men in an effort to make contact with the main body of British parachutists. He handed over his prisoners, who eventually finished up in Italian hands.

'Jungwirt had lost contact with his own headquarters, because a moutain range prevented his wireless messages getting through. So Oberstleutnant Walter Koch, CO of the German 5th Parachute Regiment, fearing the worst, set off with a relief column to search for, and assist Hans Jungwirt. In the meantime the following drama took place at the DZ, as experienced by Gavin Cadden, a veteran of Dunkirk and of the daring commando raid at Bruneval (when British parachutists dropped into occupied France, dismantled a top-secret German radar, and took it back to England). A German staff car pulled up with a full colonel of the Gestapo, Abwehr or some similar organisation. He declared the prisoners, although in British parachutist uniforms, to be saboteurs and therefore outside the protection of the Geneva Convention. He ordered their execution there and then. An Italian machine gunner was put into position. A request from Lt Buchanan to be permitted to shake hands with his men was granted, after which they were lined up against the wall in a farm yard. The farm, however, was the last known position of Jungwirt and his men. Koch, therefore, was heading for that farm. He arrived only seconds before the execution was to take place. Realising what was going on, he jumped off the still-moving vehicle, sprinted to the surprised machine gunner, kicked the gun out of its position, and shouted at the Gestapo colonel. He then turned to Lt Buchanan and his men, apologised for what had happened, secured the return of all private property which had been taken off them, and put the prisoners on to a lorry. Koch then made contact with his missing force by wireless from the farm. Being assured that his men were safe and sound, he himself went onto the back of the lorry and ordered his driver to return to his HQ, leaving the Gestapo colonel standing. In Tunis they were safely put onto an aircraft which took them to Italy.

'The main body of the 2nd Battalion suffered extremely heavy casualties during 1 December 1942. The commander, Lt-Col John Frost, decided to make a break under cover of darkness in an effort to reach British forward elements. They left, unnoticed by the enemy, in groups. However, more and more men fell by the wayside, completely exhausted. The following morning two larger groups of about 70 men each had reached two different farms in the Djebel el Mengoub area. Major

Ashford's men after refreshing themselves, settled down in a large barn offered to them by the owner, Monsieur Albert Rebourg. The exhausted men were soon sound asleep. Their rest did not last for long. A column of German motorcycle combinations, each armed with a machine gun, appeared so fast that it was impossible to wake the men. Lt Peter Stainforth did not have time to move any of the sleeping men who could not be awoken. Lt Dennis Rendell managed to mount a Bren gun in position within the barn. The leading German motorcycle entered the farmyard. Monsieur and Mademoiselle Rebourg went to meet the Germans. In the meantime the Germans on the road had taken up positions to cover their men at the farm. The crew of the leading motorcycle consisted of Lt Erich Schuster, his driver Willy Holzmann, and Gefreiter Hans Teske (the teller of this story). While Schuster and the two Rebourgs had a conversation, the Rebourgs saying that British paras had been in the farm but had since left, Teske, having caught a mild form of dysentry, quickly departed to follow the call of nature. The most suitable place was obviously behind a hay rick on the opposite side of the farm yard. Feeling better, and whilst buttoning up his trousers, he heard the sound of children's voices. In a direct line behind the young children, for whom the appearance of any soldier was exciting, within the open door of the barn stood Stainforth, his gun at the ready. Both men had to think fast. Opening fire at that moment would have

Above and right: A panzer column crosses a sizeable stream in the Tunisian hills. The Panzer III Ausf N, with the short L/24 75mm gun from the Panzer IV, was used in the close support role./*Bundesarchiv, Koblenz*

Above left: A dismounted patrol passing a column of half tracks in the hills of Tunisia. /*Bundesarchiv, Koblenz*

Left: Infantry crossing a railway line 36 kilometres from Beja Ksarbe Zougarzi. In the background is a platoon of Panzer III tanks. /*Bundesarchiv, Koblenz*

Right: An infantry patrol passes a Panzer III Ausf N in a small pass in the Tunisian hills. /*Bundesarchiv, Koblenz*

Below: A column of Panzer IIIs carrying infantry (panzer grenadiers) moving up to the front line. /*Bundesarchiv, Koblenz*

Above: Well camouflaged panzers
in a hide position.
/Bundesarchiv, Koblenz

meant the certain death of the children, probably also of the Frenchman and his daughter.
Both men thought alike and ignored each
other. In the meantime Schuster was satisfied
with the Rebourgs and the men left the farm.
Teske had to give Stainforth confidence that
he meant him no harm and put his rifle over
his shoulder. A most uncomfortable ride for
him, for he could not be sure if Stainforth
would not act like a bully at school who hits
his opponent once his back is turned.

'Teske had no idea that there were about
74 men in the barn, Stainforth had no idea
that German armour was just beyond a hill.
One thing is certain, had either man lost his
nerve, a terrible massacre would have taken
place, with almost certain death for all
who were in the farm, British, German,
French and Tunisians. The farm,
called Abbaci Farm is still standing today
as it did in 1942, and is impossible to
defend'.

Action at Sidi bou Zid

It was now the turn of the Axis to take the
offensive and both von Arnim's and Rommel's forces launched attacks in the direction
of the Kasserine Pass. *Frühlingswind* (Spring
Breeze) was the first of these and was launched through the Faid Pass onto Sidi bou Zid
on 14 February by von Arnim's 10th and 21st
Panzer Divisions. Operation *Morgenluft*
(Morning Air) was launched two days later
by the DAK, through Gafsa. Rommel's aim
was to cause maximum casualties and destruction to the inexperienced American
forces, with all the resulting effects on their
morale and future fighting ability. If their
luck held the German forces might even be
able to cut right behind the Allied lines and

destroy their main bases at Bone and Constantine.

Unfortunately for the Germans and for
Rommel in particular, as this was clearly to be
his last chance to 'pull the chestnuts out of the
fire', their plans had the germ of failure within
them from the outset. Rommel and von
Arnim heartily disliked each other – they
were complete opposites, von Arnim an aris-
tocrat from the established officer class, hated
the 'upstart Swabian'. In addition there was
little or no co-ordination between the two
armies, *Heeresgruppe Afrika* not being formed
until 23 February, and without this unified
command there was little chance of much
lasting success.

To illustrate this battle I have chosen an
extract from the privately published history
of Machine Gun Battalion 8, who were the
third battalion of Infanterie Regiment 104 in
21 Panzer Division. Their part in the opening
battles of Operation *Frühlingswind* is described
thus:

'Our battalion marched off on 13 February
with 21 Panzer Division who had been relieved of the Faid Pass by 10 Panzer Division.
We pushed through Gunifidia southwards,
swinging round Sidi Mecheri, then north-
west to Bir el Afey on the main road from
Gafsa to Sidi bou Zid. Moving on from there
we reached a dried out wadi west of Zaafria
(about 14km west of Sidi bou Zid) by the
early morning of 14 February.

'Our division had gone round Sidi bou Zid
far to the south and stood west of it on the
communicating lines between the two American concentrations at Sidi bou Zid and
Gafsa. On the edge of this wadi the division
took up a position with front northwards.
In front of the position all was quiet. In-

Above right: Part of a panzer grenadier platoon pauses for a brief smoke break in the hills of Tunisia./*Bundesarchiv, Koblenz*

Right: Last of the tanks to appear in North Africa was the E version of the Tiger. Only one battalion of these famous tanks with their deadly 88mm guns was sent to Tunisia./*Bundesarchiv, Koblenz*

Below: German infantrymen passing through the battered Tunisian town of Terbourba /*Associated Press*

definable noises drifted down to us from the distance. At about 0100 our eyes jumped out of their sockets and we caught our breath as a huge wedge of tanks came towards us. Undaunted 1 Company's new 7.5 cm anti-tank gun started the battle. Unfortunately it hadn't been very well camouflaged and the clouds of dust that each round threw up gave away its position. After a short exchange of fire it was knocked out by two direct hits.

'Now the Americans knew our positions and they halted. Either they overestimated our strength or they lacked an aggressive instinct. Our artillery used this hesitation to lay down a barrage, during which, tanks of 5 and 7 Regiments (the latter from 10 Panzer Division) pushed right and left of the thickly bunched American tanks under cover of the tall cacti. Then all hell broke loose!

'Our *Panzerschutzen* fired shot after shot; yelling and explosions filled the air; tanks were burning, enveloped by dense clouds of black smoke, while others exploded, and some turned in circles, with one track destroyed, aimlessly firing all the while. Then the Luftwaffe joined in the attack and the inferno mounted – a picture of hell right before our eyes. . . .'

In the middle of this 'picture of hell' was Sgt Clarence W. Coley, radio operator of a Sherman tank named *Texas*, the battalion command tank of the 3rd Battalion, 1st US

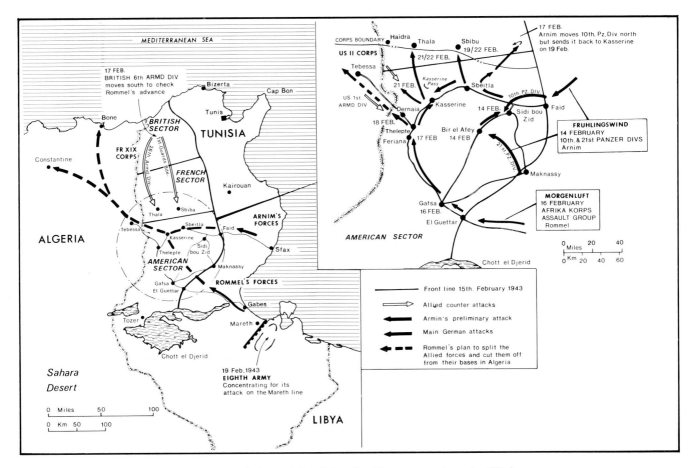

Armored Regiment, which was commanded by Lt-Col Louis V. Hightower. In *The Battle History of the 1st Armored Division* (the 'Old Ironsides') he tells what happened to his tank in the attack:

'February 14th, 1943 started off just like any other of those beautiful African days we had been having there in the "cactus patch" near Sidi bou Zid for the past week or so. We had been taking it easy, knowing the enemy was over there, somewhere the other side of Faid Pass. The evening before, at officers' call, we had been instructed to dig holes, deep holes, to sleep in because of reports of big guns moving into position to shell us. I, like the rest, slept as well as ever because everything was quiet that night.

'When daybreak came on that fatal morning we crawled out of our holes for our first "stand-to," which meant checking equipment, motors, radios, and guns. I climbed into the turret of the Battalion command tank, an M4 named *Texas*, the vehicle of which I was a crew member. I turned on the SCR-508 radio, checking it for operation, and it checked out OK. I then got out of the turret and into the assistant driver's seat, and turned on the SCR-245, which was mounted in the right sponson. It was OK also. In the meantime, Clark, the driver, had started up the motor, and about that time, here comes Col Hightower with brief case in hand. Climbing into the turret, he tells Clark to move out.

'The Colonel told me to get into the CC A net. I proceeded to report into the net and took over from the set which was installed in the Battalion command track as Battalion command station. We moved on out and after a short time, stopped near CC A Headquarters tent, leaving us sitting there wondering what it was all about. In the meantime, Companies H and I were pulling out of bivouac area and getting in position on the road. I think that is about the time when I learned that the Germans had attacked Company G, which was in position at a place called the "Oasis".

'After a short time the Colonel came out of the Headquarters and mounted the tank and we moved out. He got the company commanders of H and I Companies lined out, and we took off towards the "Oasis." We hadn't gone very far when we ran into blistering fire from many guns, including a lot of "Eighty-eights," I suppose. I didn't see too much and didn't know much about what was going on, but I did see many of our tanks get hit. Somtimes two or three men got out. Sometimes no one got out. Most of the tanks burned when hit. The artillery got so hot and heavy, and we were losing so many tanks due to being outranged, that the Colonel decided to withdraw. So we started backing out, keeping our thickest armor toward the enemy. The Colonel told Clark to back and zig-zag, and when we reached a suitable place, to turn fast and get going. I remember that two men got on our tanks to ride out of the battle area—but I guess we were moving too slow for them because pretty soon they jumped to the ground and took off on foot.

'We moved on back towards Sidi bou Zid, and learned by radio that the Germans had put up a road block there and we were expecting to have to fight our way through it. I loaded my .30-cal. machine gun and was ready to fire at anything that looked suspicious but the road block did not materialize, so I did not get to fire. Back in Sidi bou Zid we pulled in beside a building and the Colonel left us on foot to check the situation. As we had started before breakfast that morning, Clark, Bayer, Agee and I warmed up some C-rations and had us a feast. It was around noon, anyway.

'Pretty soon the Colonel came back to the tank. We mounted up and moved out towards the desert. I didn't know in what direction but away from the enemy which had all but wiped us out. The Luftwaffe paid us many visits that day. They seemed to have about a 20-minute schedule, just time enough to go back and load up again. It was getting up in the afternoon now, and was pretty hot and smoky in this whole area. As we were moving along, we could see many other vehicles moving in the same general direction across the desert, half-tracks, peeps, motorcycles, and trucks. About five tanks of Company H had moved on out ahead of us. As far as we knew, we were the only tank back there, and the Colonel seemed to want to bring up the rear, keeping between the enemy and our withdrawing forces.

'As we were moving along, I suddenly got a call on my SCR-245 set. I answered telling Capt Green to go ahead with his message. His message was to the effect that a bunch of German tanks were shooting up the column, knocking out trucks and half-tracks, one after the other. I put the message on a message blank and passed it up into the turret to Col Hightower, who immediately got on the SCR-508 set and tried to contact the tanks of H Company, which he knew were ahead of us. But no luck – he could not raise a peep from any of them.

'The Colonel then said we would just have to take them on by ourselves. He immediately rotated the turret until the 75mm was pointing over the left rear fender at the German tanks. I don't remember when I first found out that there were seven of them. Perhaps Larry Green had it in the message. But anyhow, Cpl Bayer, the gunner, started firing at them. Col Hightower was observing the fire with field glasses. I could hear him complimenting Bayer on getting hits. Clark, the driver, was craning his neck trying to see the action. Agee, the loader, was busy keeping

104

the 75 loaded. All the time we were firing at the Supermen, they were not wasting any time. We were getting it hot and heavy. I did not keep the count on them, but we received many hits on our tank. I could feel the shock and hear the loud noise as those projectiles bounced off.

'We had done quite a bit of firing that morning over towards Faid Pass, and the rounds were running out in the turret racks, but we had a few rounds left in the racks underneath the turret. So I took off my head-phones, laid them up on the BC-312 receiver, took the back of the assistant driver's seat out, and placed it up front under the .30-cal machine gun, very deliberately. I had no fear, and was calm and collected. It is when you have nothing to do that you are afraid. Sitting backwards on my seat, with my feet on the escape hatch, I began pulling the rounds from the racks underneath the turret, and passing them up to Agee, the loader. I remember that other times when I had needed to take rounds from those racks, it was very hard for me to get them out because I was afraid of hurting my fingers, but believe me this time those rounds came out easy. I didn't worry about my fingers. In fact, I wouldn't have given two cents for our chances to get out of that mess alive. I kept passing the

ammo, Agee kept loading, and Bayer kept firing that 75. Every once in a while I could hear the Colonel tell Bayer that he had hit another.

'Our luck finally ran out. A round got stuck in the gun, wouldn't go in or come out. I remember that I had about three rounds lying on the turret floor when the round got stuck, so I got straightened back up in my seat. The Colonel told Clark to move on out, and about the same time, one of the guns got a penetration in our tank. The projectile came in the left side, passing through the gas tank, ricocheting around, and winding up on the escape hatch just behind my seat. Thirty seconds earlier I was bent over in that space pulling ammo from the racks. I re-member it well – sitting there watching that bit of hell standing on end, spinning like a top, with fire flying out of the upper part of it like it was a tracer. Our tank was on fire inside.

'I heard the Colonel say: "Let's get the hell out of here." So we started bailing out. I distinctly remember trying three times to raise my hatch, but it wouldn't go up but about four inches on account of that part of the turret which contained the radio over-hanging the hatch. The Colonel, Clark, Bayer, and Agee were all out of the tank while I'm

Above: Paratroops pause for a quick smoke in a palm lined street. Note the jump smocks worn on top of normal uniform. /*Bundesarchiv, Koblenz*

Top left: Briefing an ambush party. Note the two Teller anti-tank mines on the left of the picture and the Model 24 stick type hand grenades carried on top of the entrenching tool and bayonet./*Bundesarchiv, Koblenz*

Bottom left: A US Army outpost on a hillside in Tunisia grimly awaits a counter-attack by the Afrika Korps./*IWM*

trying to get my hatch open. I finally gave up trying to get my hatch open and got across the transmission like a snake and up through the driver's hatch, diving head first out of that burning vehicle. Hitting the ground on my shoulders, I rolled over and before I got to my feet, I noticed the tracks were burning also. I jumped to my feet and took off after the rest of the crew, who were not letting any grass grow under their feet. When I was between 25 and 50 yards away, I heard an explosion. Looking back, I could see fire shooting skywards from old *Texas*, ammo or gas blowing up, I suppose.

'I caught up with the other fellows in short order. The Colonel instructed us to scatter out a little, but I can't remember if we did or not. My total equipment at that time consisted of a tank helmet, a pair of coveralls, and a combat jacket with a busted zipper. I had left my pistol in my foxhole that morning when I had gone to check my radio, never dreaming that we were going to get into the worst battle of all time that very day. We moved on across the desert on foot, sweating out small arms fire from the German tanks, but I guess it was so smoky and dusty that they couldn't see us. We were also sweating out the Arabs because, although I may be wrong, I don't believe any of us were armed.

'We tried to signal some passing vehicles but no luck. They were quite a distance away. After a half hour or so of walking and running, we came across two half-tracks, one of which was broken down. The Colonel advised the crews of the situation and suggested that they had better load up and get out of there because the German tanks were not far away and heading in our direction. A member of one of the half-track crews had a very nasty wound in his side, and had been bleeding a lot, but they had already put sulfa powder and bandages on the wound, and he was doing OK. We stripped the broken down track of its machine guns, and took the men's personal belongings and put them in the other track, along with the wounded man, and all climbed aboard and took off, leaving the broken down track sit. We didn't burn it because we had expectations of coming back and picking it up, so they said. You can't prove it by me.

We made it on back beyond Kern's Crossroads (which had not been named yet) to an assembly area on a piece of high ground.'

To return to the German narrative:
'In the evening 34 Shermans lay burnt out or still smouldering redly. We combed the area and took 3 officers and 74 men prisoner, most of whom belonged to the 1st US Armoured Division and were in action for the first time. They sat down in holes in the road and immediately went to sleep.
'The tank battle on our front continued on the 15th. Gradually the enemy were pushed back north-westwards, losing on the two days about 150 tanks and armoured vehicles and about 2,000 men taken prisoner. Unfortunately this success wasn't followed up by an immediate attack on Sbeitla. Rommel would regret that later. After our battalion had spent the 16th near Sidi Bou Zid without being troubled by the enemy, we were ordered to join up with the advancing division on the Faid Pass–Sbeitla road early on the 17th.

'We marched away from Sidi bou Zid in darkness. The track led north-westwards about 5 km away from the parallel main road to Sbeitla. At dawn we turned right to join up immediately with the division's route. The

formation at the front of the column under the commander of 3 Company, the young and intense Lt Boy who was always pushing forward, lost contact with us in the dark. Hauptmann Kuhn therefore sent forward Unteroffizier Kurth from the Signals Platoon with Gefreiter Schäfer and a captured jeep to re-establish communications and to tell him where the battalion was.

'Driving at the head of the battalion's column was a *Schutzenpanzerwagen**, the only one at the disposal of our Panzergrenadier Batallion. The adjutant (Lt Starke) sat at his machine gun, watching the land surrounding the track from his vantage point. Suddenly, in the distance to the right front, he saw movements of at first single figures and then groups. They couldn't be made out distinctly on the cactus and thorn crowded slopes, but it was clear that they were moving from left to right and therefore getting close to the battalion's route.

'Then Starke saw that the jeep with Unteroffizier Kurth was getting ever closer – obviously on its return journey. Shots came from the place he had seen the movement and all at once the jeep was surrounded by a group of men, whose olive coloured combat clothing and spherical helmets showed them clearly to be Americans.

'Alarm! Shooting was impossible at that moment for fear of endangering the crew of the jeep. Hauptmann Kuhn was told of the strength of the enemy and he sent 1 and 3 Companies, who had been at the head of the

column, left of the track to stop any further movement west by the enemy. Oberleutnant Batt, with 5 Company who were quite far back, was immediately sent right of the track at the start of the fight to take the enemy in the flank. Lt Starke roared off in the SPW to save, if possible, the crew of the jeep, to hold down the enemy, and to keep them occupied until the battalion had disembarked from its vehicles and moved up, and the lead platoon had come back. As the SPW moved off Lt Starke opened fire forcing the Americans to go to cover. He found the jeep, but it was empty. Lt Boy and the head of the column had already reached the main road, and at this point Lt Starke came upon a company of 5 Panzer Regiment, resting, and their commander lent him two tanks. With these and Lt Boy he advanced southwards down the track. The shooting had become widespread. Both sides lay opposite each other, firing at point blank range. The enemy were obviously considerably extended and exasperated at having their advance checked, yet they made little attempt to break out of cover. It was only when Starke ferreted the Americans out of their hiding places, either singly or in groups, by driving all over the place in the SPW and winkling them out with machine gun fire that the battalion could move forward and get to grips with them. While Starke was doing this, the enemy repeatedly tried to knock out the SPW with short range weapons, but didn't manage it. Perhaps they were exhausted by the heavy battles of the last few days. Lt Starke could hardly believe his eyes as more and more gave themselves up as the engagement continued into the afternoon. Altogether 47 officers and 731 men surrendered. The majority came from an engineer battalion of either the 1st US Armoured Division or II US Corps. However, the large number of officers showed that other units must also have been represented. Mentioned in the Battalion's reports as the senior ranking prisoner was a Colonel Drake.*

'. . . Drake had wanted to break through to Sbeitla with his battalion, to connect up again with his own forces. They looked at us mistrustfully, but as we obviously weren't the barbarians their propaganda had made out, relations soon relaxed. They got cigarettes out of the capacious pockets of their practical combat jackets. . . . The Americans were astounded at our small numbers – we were only a paltry 300 men – and couldn't understand how we had captured them.

Schutzenpanzerwagen (SPW): An armoured personnel carrier employed by the German Army for a wide variety of roles. As an APC it could carry 10 men in addition to its normal crew of two and was armed with two machine guns, one at the front with an armoured shield and one at the back on an AA bracket.

*Colonel Thomas D. Drake was the commanding officer of 168th Infantry Regiment and had received the Silver Star from General Eisenhower at Sidi bou Zid only a few hours before the German attack through the Faid Pass began.

'By combing the area Kurth and Schäfer were found. They lay not far from the jeep behind a thicket of cactus. Both were dead from stomach wounds. Incredible – both dead from identical wounds. Kurth was one of the original members of the battalion. Two years of uninterrupted service in North Africa lay behind him, from the start of the North African campaign, and before that he had served in Poland and France. He had been sometime leader of the radio troop of the 1st Platoon and had been, at the time of his death, with the Signals Platoon. He was a particularly painful loss. Kurth and his companion Schäfer were our only dead on that day and they were laid beside the American casualties on the main road.

'On the same day the division had taken Sbeitla after a short battle. We did not leave until the 18th, so as to be able to make this area safe to the north and north-west. A large battle patrol under Lt Boy was sent to Kasserine with two light machine guns, one heavy machine gun and an anti-tank gun. On his route he found a crash-landed USAF aeroplane belonging to the US Air Force and near it the crew. Then he continued, reached Kasserine which he found to be free of enemy, let himself be entertained hospitably by the population, after which he returned swiftly.

'On 19 February, 104 Regiment undertook an advance on Sbiba, 35km north of Sbeitla, the same target as 21 Panzer Division. While III Battalion under Hauptmann Kurzai made a feint attack along the road, the 3rd and 5th Companies crossed a wide wadi on the right of the road and went well forward towards Sbiba. However there was a universal order to halt in the evening. The night brought rain, softening up the ground, and at dawn the battalion was brought back. It was not until later that morning that the attack was renewed, this time with 50 tanks from the 5th Regiment, with I Battalion on the right. It was a miserable grind in countryside that became quite mountainous. In spite of this we went forward practically uninterrupted. The tanks gave fire support against an obviously weakened enemy, following the battalion from sector to sector. However, around midday, the countryside about 7km in front of Sbiba narrowed into a form of pass. It became steeper and steeper on either side, the walls traversed by ravines. The tanks couldn't follow any more and stayed back. The battalion advanced about 1km in the face of ever increasing defensive fire and then the attack stopped. Towards midnight the battalion was withdrawn about 100m to get it out of the worst field of fire.

'At break of day on 21 February the battalion took up a position on a barren, stony hill, unfortunately a few minutes late. As the

companies reached the top it became light and the enemy artillery hit us with a heavy barrage that made any movement impossible. Luckily we found a number of Arab storage cellars, cut deeply into the stony ground, and they gave us good cover. The artillery fire went on all day and showed us once more the surplus of munitions at the enemy's disposal. In the evening we cleared off the heights. In the valley stood an old Arab with a fluttering burnus. He embraced some of us, murmuring "Salaam" and "Allah il Allah", and blessed us. Would the blessing help? It was almost incomprehensible how much fellow feeling the Arab population of Tunisia showed us. We stayed around Sbeitla for three days, alternatively attacked by fighter-bombers and pounded by artillery.

The Battle History of the 1st US Armoured Division sums up the action at Sidi bo Zid with the words:
'It was hard for the Division to realize that on two successive days the 3d and 2d Battalions, 1st Armoured Regiment, and a considerable portion of the Division artillery had been chewed up by enemy ground and air forces. "We might have walloped them or they might have walloped us," General Ward reported to General Fredenall at about 2230 hours. Eventually the bitter truth was accepted: the troops on the hills around Sidi-bou-Zid were still marooned, surrounded by an enemy force of great power. The Division had been "walloped".'

1st Armoured had learnt a bitter lesson the hard way, but it was one they were never to forget as their splendid battle record in Italy clearly shows. For the victors there was little to celebrate, as the initiative so tenaciously

Above: A wounded Afrika Korps officer gets ready to be taken off to the POW cage./*IWM*

Above right: Generalmajor Freiherr von Liebenstein surrendering to General Freyberg at HQ 10 Corps on 13 May 1943. /*Maj W. Burshall*

Left: Maresciallo d'Italia di Armata Messe, commander of 1 *italienische Armee*, surrendering to General Freyberg. When General Messe took over from Rommel on 23 February 1943, German divisions came under Italian field command for the very first time. Messe was promoted to Field Marshal on 13 May 1943, the last day of the campaign in Africa. /*Maj W. Bursnall*

Below: The shock of defeat was too much for this utterly dejected soldier./*IWM*

Bottom: Acres of prisoners. German and Italian prisoners wait in the Tunisian sunshine for transportation to permanent POW camps./*IWM*

gained was frittered away. The offensive had started off with great promise, and yet had carried the germ of failure within itself: firstly the movements of Rommel's armoured forces and Von Arnim's 5th Panzerarmee had not been synchronised; then the Italian command had fixed the attack objectives so badly that Rommel had run into the enemy reserves; and, finally, Montgomery was active from 17 February. He ventured a couple of attacks on the Mareth line with the 51st Highland Division and 7th Armoured Division and quickly sent the rest of his forces in Libya to the front. So Rommel's attacks on the line Sbiba – Thala and Tebessa had miscarried. The enemy were too superior in anti-tank weapons and artillery and had increased in strength almost visibly in the air.

Surrender

After the failure of the Kasserine battle Rommel wearily turned back to face Montgomery, who was now preparing to assault the Mareth Line, the last real line of defence left to the DAK. In what has been described as one of his most skilful tactical battles Montgomery and his Eighth Army eventually broke through, but did not really exploit their success, thereby allowing the DAK to disengage and retreat to the north. But the ultimate end of the Axis in North Africa was by now a foregone conclusion. Mid April found them reduced to holding a tight perimeter in the last range of hills which surrounds the coastal plain around Bizerta and Tunis. Rommel, faced with surrender or annihilation, flew back to Germany to beg for his gallant army to be evacuated, but Hitler was determined that there should be no surrender. He also forbade Rommel the opportunity of returning, so that when the

moment of surrender finally came he was not in North Africa. No doubt he felt the humiliation just as deeply as did his defeated soldiers. Here is how one of them, Werner Susek, remembers the final surrender of his artillery battery:

'May 1943: The third battery of the Artillery Regiment 190 has been in well fortified positions for a few weeks near Enfidafille in Tunisia. The battery keeps on firing day and night. At night it sustains barrage-fire upon attacking English infantry. The ammunition is sometimes bad. One day a gun barrel burst and the gunners were wounded. Afterwards the barrel looked like a peeled banana. The English return our fire with heavy guns that make our dug-outs quake. On the first day of Easter they attack with over a hundred bombers. Luckily for us the bombs are dropped short, but one man is killed in a neighbouring unit. Nevertheless life is somewhat more agreeable than it was in the summer of 1942 during the push through the desert. Someone has supplied us with Tunisian wine, but as a few comrades get rather tight, the wine is forbidden. Then comes the day when we hear artillery fire to our rear. Officially we are informed by our battery officer that we have been cut off by the enemy, but have to go on fighting until the end. On our left there is the Mediterranean Sea, on our right there are the mountains, the Tommies are in front of us and in the rear. The mess is complete then. Two guns are turned and point towards the enemy in the rear. On 10 May we are challenged by the English general opposite us to surrender. He assures us of good treatment and everyone is supposed to take only two blankets with him. The challenge is declined and after the expiration of the ultimatum the English shellfire increases. The 12th of May is the decisive day. In the morning the English begin with heavy artillery and tank fire which we violently return. At noon the English in front of us fire with smoke-shells to indicate our positions for their attacking bombers. The attack causes damage only to some trucks, but the regimental headquarters suffer a number of dead and wounded. Thereafter more heavy shell-fire. Finally in the afternoon we receive the expected signal: "Scapa Flow", the sign to blow up our guns and surrender. We climb out of our dugouts, waving white towels. The English cease fire immediately. For the last time the third battery falls in as on parade. The staff-sergeant says a few words about "comradeship and endurance" etc. The insufferable tension of the preceding days reaches its climax as we see the first English. They are coming on motorcycles, on jeeps, escorted by swarms of infantrymen. The vehicles stop and the Tommies approach with pointed guns. They also set up a light

machine gun. A very young English officer gets out of the first jeep. He moves towards out battery officer. The latter lifts his right hand to his cap and reports the battery ready for surrender and assures on his word of honour that we do not possess any weapons. The Englishman also salutes and they both shake hands. Our officer offers cigarettes. We are ordered to break ranks. And then something happens we have scarcely expected. The English infantrymen move towards us and when they join us they shake hands with us. Photos of relatives are shown to each other. There isn't the least indication of hostility. Suddenly the order: *Achtung!* Everybody stands to attention. The English as well. Our divisional Commander passes by. His car stops and he salutes: "*Heil, Kanoniere*". We answer: "*Heil, Herr general*".

'Then we say goodbye to the English and drive in our own trucks in the direction of the prison camp. Our late enemies keep on waving their hands for a long time. On the road to Tunis we meet lots of trucks full of English troops. Each time we wave to each other. Who is to be envied? For us the war is finished, for them it will begin again. On the second day of our captivity the English guards of Camp Tunis challenge us to a football match. A team is formed and the English lose 3:2. They demand revenge and on the following day they lose 4:2. Both matches

Above: Generaloberst Jürgen von Arnim, *Heeresgruppe* commander, who took over from Rommel on 9 March 1943, seen here after surrendering at noon on 12 May 1943./*IWM*

Left: A panzer burns on the outskirts of Tunis, close to a German graveyard./*IWM*

Below: Despondent and yet defiant, a striking study of a prisoner of war, taken in Tunisia in April 1943./*IWM*

were absolutely fair. For all of us this was a magnificent event that happened in the midst of the war, during a period when the press on both sides of the Channel was preaching hate and bloodlust.

'Life in a prison camp is not a holiday. The coming months were severe. Food was scarce and the climate was gnawing at us. There were, inevitably, provocations between those who guard and those who are guarded. After staying in several prison camps we were taken to the USA where we were to stay for a long time. On 24 August 1943, we left Oran in convoy of about 60 vessels escorted by aircraft carriers and destroyers. Nearly two years of hardship under the glowing sun and ceaseless fighting in the desert were over.'

The Afrika Korps Surrenders
The most notable surrender was of course that of the Afrika Korps. Just before mid-night on 12 May 1943, their commander, General Cramer, sent out a last signal:
'Ammunition shot off. Arms and equipment destroyed. In accordance with orders received the Afrika Korps has fought itself to the con-dition where it can fight no more. The German Afrika Korps must rise again. *Heia Safari!*

Cramer, General Commanding'

The Dead and the Living

The Debris of War
'No landscape à la Goya. Here no teees
Uprooted, gutted farms; the unsalvaged scrap
The scattered petrol-cans, the upturned
And abandoned truck, the fallen Heinkel; all
The rusted and angular detritus
Of war'.

So wrote Jocelyn Brooke in his poem *Landscape near Tobruk*. It is of course hardly surprising to learn that the face of the Western Desert was scattered with the flotsam and jetsam of modern war when one considers how many bitter battles took place there. Some shot up, some burnt out, the trucks, tanks, armoured cars, guns and planes lay together with smaller debris on the battlefields. And in so many places as well there were the crosses, some of wood and some of stone, marking the last resting places of those who had paid the supreme sacrifice. The photo-graphs in this section show all types of casualties, both to men and material. The more fortunate, lightly damaged ones were mended so that they could be used again – the vehicles in repair shops like the one I have featured elsewhere in this book; the men too in their own 'repair shops', where the surgeon's skill replaced that of the vehicle mechanic. In these hospitals the German Red Cross nurses braved the bombs and shells to help with the wounded, and four nurses were awarded the Iron Cross for heroic services.

Wounded at Tobruk
The following short article appeared in *Signal* – the German military propaganda magazine – in November 1941:
' "There are not many casualties at Tobruk at present", writes our reporter. "The German soldier here knows his opponent too

Below: German graves near El Adem 1942./*H. Green*

Top right: A group of Afrika Korps graves in the desert marking the site of yet another bloody engagement./*H. Auger*

Centre right: More German graves./*K. Popplewell*

Bottom right: Laying two comrades to rest in shallow desert graves.
/*Bundesarchiv, Koblenz*

well. He is familiar with the tricks of the Australian reconnaissance troops who feint an attack to the left and then come in on the right. He knows which parts of the country the British like to bombard and the artillery knows how long it takes before the enemy answers our fire. If he shoots with the 7.5cm guns, they know it by the clear sound of the firing and there is plenty of time to take cover. About 15 seconds. The howitzers are quicker. You hear the firing and the screaming of the shell immediately follows. Then you have to jump. The soldiers here are old hands who know all this. The care of the wounded in positional warfare such as this is, naturally functions without friction. The hospital tents lie not far beyond the range of the British guns. They are equipped with all the installations for first aid and are fitted with double and triple walls to keep out the sandstorms. The planes which convey the wounded to the hospitals in the towns start and land quite close to them. The names of the doctors there are famous in Germany. University professors are among them. They are helped by nurses who have now been carrying out their strenuous duties for months on end in the unaccustomed climate. They are worshipped by the soldiers'.

Reinforcements

For every casualty there should have been a replacement sent up, but of course this was not always possible. When they did arrive it

was not always easy to assimilate them – here
is how Lt Ralph Ringler remembers reinforcements arriving:

'Meanwhile night had fallen and it was pitch
black when I was told that 14 men had arrived
as replacements. A lorry had just brought
them up from Battalion. I groped my way
over to the vehicle and looked at this wind-
fall. With an almost totally dim pocket torch
I lit up their faces and mounds of luggage –
these 14 had more equipment than the whole
of the rest of the company! Seven NCO's and
seven panzer grenadiers, of these only four
were actual replacements. Quickly I called
over the platoon and group commanders to
me and gave them each a couple of men. I
impressed on them that the new men could
keep only that equipment which was absolutely necessary. The superfluous things
must go back with the field kitchen. The
Feldwebel (Company Sergeant Major) with
the new men seemed to me to be a braggart
and I had to talk to him very uncivilly. The
worst thing about it was that these men in
their new uniforms and without personal
loyalty, were put into the middle of an
experience the end of which they could not
see. Before I sent them to their groups and
platoons I went from man to man and learnt
his name. Meanwhile the front had broken
up again, all around us shells had begun to
drop, and tanks on both sides showed that
they were also still alive. The new men were

quickly sent off and also the field kitchen, along with the lorry and the water truck'.

Capture and Escape

For some soldiers to be taken prisoner in battle meant interminable months or even years in a prisoner of war camp. Others were more fortunate and perhaps the two short stories I have chosen about being taken prisoner serve to highlight the vagaries of capture in North Africa, where chance played an even greater part than normal in events.

Karl Susenberger, a radio operator in 104 Panzer Grenadier Regiment, was taken prisoner briefly by the British during a battle in late June 1942 over a strongpoint near the Egyptian frontier, whilst the Afrika Korps was pressing on victoriously towards the final British positions near El Alamein. Tobruk had just fallen and his spirits, like those of everyone else in his unit, were high. The attack on the strongpoint was going well and Susenberger with his comrades was some 200 metres away from the British wire, when they were counter-attacked by tanks. His radio van was damaged and immobilised, the next moment he was surrounded by the enemy:

'A Tommy looked into my vehicle with his sub-machine gun threatening – "Hands up!" he cried. I was so shocked that I just looked up at him and couldn't move. Suddenly he fired and put a burst into the wireless. That broke the tension and I obeyed his order to get out. As I dismounted I saw our other vehicles about 100 metres away driving off – they had left me. At once a couple of Tommies searched me – they really took me to pieces! I had to take everything off, even my underclothes. In the radio car they had found all the signals documents – we had received weighty instructions that these shouldn't fall into enemy hands – so what, I couldn't do anything about it. I was then taken to their position where I had to wait in front of a tent. The sentry gave me a cigarette, but I couldn't taste it, I couldn't really latch onto the fact that I had been taken prisoner. After about 10 minutes I was led into the tent and found myself in front of an officer; he spoke some German and asked me how old I was, I answered that I was 19. He had my paybook in his hand: "You belong to the 21st Panzer Division, Third Battalion, Regiment 104". I acknowledged this fact. He produced the signals documents and asked if I was a radio operator, again I replied in the affirmative, then he said that we would talk about this later. I was taken outside once more and led over to a heavy lorry. By the last rays of the sun I could see that the Tommies were loading up their lorries, they obviously wanted to leave the strongpoint. They took up their marching positions with two sentries next to me. They talked non-stop and took hardly any notice of me. After a few minutes the

Top left: Graves near Sollum. /H. Auger

Centre left: Lonely graves in the heart of the Western Desert. /H. I. Turner

Below, far left: The grave of a British airman near Tobruk close to his burnt out and wrecked aircraft./Col W. Kaulback

Below left: Afrika Korps graves outside Tobruk./Col W. Kaulback

Below: A grave close to a demolished German half track. The letter E denotes that it has been completely destroyed by the Sappers./IWM

Above left: The long road into captivity. Italian prisoners taken in Tobruk during its initial capture in 1940./*Col de Salis*

Above: Italian prisoners outside Tobruk 1940 – they look remarkably cheerful./*Col de Salis*

Left: Axis prisoners, taken in Bardia, waiting to embark into lighters at Sollum, whence they will be ferried out to waiting ships to take them to POW camps far away./*IWM*

Below left: Indian prisoners taken in the May 1942 offensive near Tobruk./*Col T. Bock*

Above right: British prisoners help bandage wounded comrades. /*Bundesarchiv, Koblenz*

Right: 'For you the war is over!' British POW taken by the Afrika Korps./*Bundesarchiv, Koblenz*

column began to move. We had been driving for about a quarter of an hour when suddenly a hurricane of fire broke on us. I never experienced one of a similar intensity again in Africa. Immediately we jumped out of the vehicles and hit the deck. I lay between the back wheels and saw the big explosions of the 88's shells, the tracers of the 2cm guns and the machine gun fire. It couldn't have been worse in Hell. The first lorries were set on fire and the screams of the wounded pierced me to the quick. Total confusion reigned and I saw the Tommies running about in all directions. When I looked around there was nothing to be seen of my two guards. That gave me the chance to escape and I crept slowly away from the lorry. Outside everything was illuminated by the glare of a burning flare. I simply ran for it and after some hundred metres fell into a hole almost on top of an Englishman. His scream of pain was loud as I almost fell on his back, I said "Shut

up!'' and immediately got hold of his weapon. It was no usual trench that we lay in, it was much bigger. When the excitement had died down a bit I offered the Tommy a cigarette, which he took. He spoke a few sentences to me but I didn't understand. We sat like that until dawn, then, when some of our men came into the area I made myself known. A lieutenant of the Light Anti Aircraft Battalion 18 took us into custody and I explained to him what had happened. "Good Lord" he said, "you had a hell of a time – which unit do you belong to?"

"Third Battalion, 104", I said. He told me he would try to get me and my prisoner back to my battalion. I now saw many other English-men who had been taken prisoner by my comrades and I realised how lucky I'd been in the whole affair.

'After a few hours I was driven to the battalion where I reported to Hauptmann Reissman with the words, "Lance Corporal Susenberger with a prisoner back from the English prison camp". I also reported the loss of my paybook and signals documents.

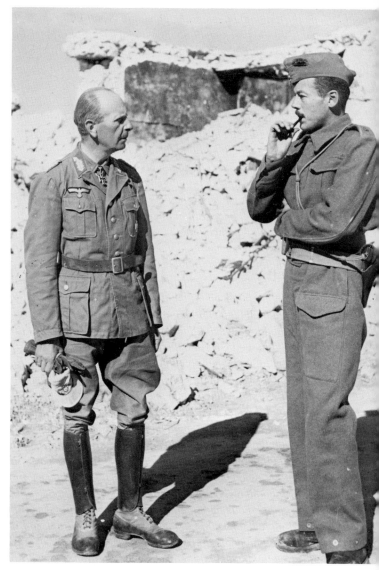

Left: Water being distributed among British prisoners of war. /IWM

Below, far left: British prisoners of war making sandwiches for distribution to their comrades. /IWM

Below left: General Johann Von Ravenstein, commander of 21 Panzer Division, who was captured by the New Zealanders on 29 November 1941, pictured here with his escort officer. /IWM

Right: Gunner Ubbe was hit at 7am. The British answered the German troops' morning greeting with a salvo from the 7.5cm guns and Ubbe did not manage to take cover in time. His foot was bandaged with a field dressing and by 9am. he was being lifted into the plane which will take him to the hospital. (Published in *Signal* magazine, and reproduced here by kind permission of the Imperial War Museum.)/*Eileen Tweedy*

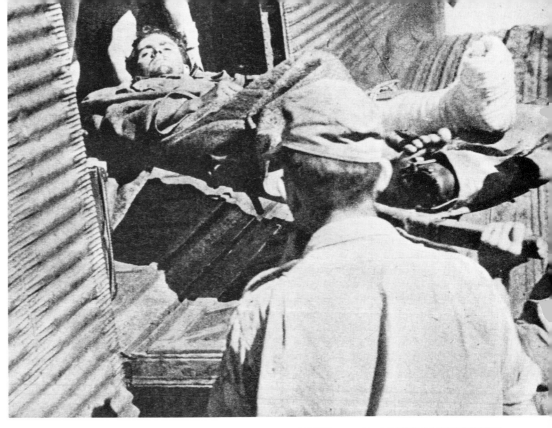

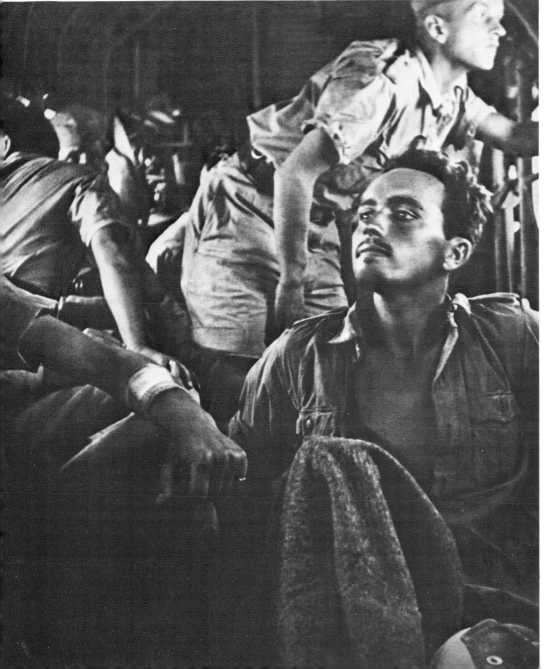

Above: Soothing hands. Gunner Ubbe has not seen any women for three months. There are only soldiers at Tobruk. As fate would have it, the first woman he sees is the nurse in the hospital who holds his head during the operation. (Published in *Signal* magazine and reproduced here by kind permission of the IWM.) /*Eileen Tweedy*

Left: A town in sight, white houses and trees . . . The plane with the wounded men on board is approaching its destination. The flight took them across the sea. Now they see the coast and the white town on the edge of the sea. The soldiers gaze spellbound at the unaccustomed sight. (Published in *Signal* magazine, and reproduced here by kind permission of the Imperial War Museum.) /*Eileen Tweedy*

119

Captain Reissman greeted me with a hand shake and said "That is of course a bit of a bloody nuisance but it's good that you're back". I had to write a report about the loss of my paybook etc, and later I had to recount all the details of my escape with the Tommy'.

The second short story is about the capture of two British officers by a reconnaissance patrol of AA3 – the recce battalion of 15 Panzer Division – in November 1941, when the British were on the offensive. Major Curt Ehle, who sent me the story, was at the time attached to Divisional Headquarters. He had been in charge of a small recce and battle planning team during the preparations for Rommel's initial attack on Tobruk. However, when this proved abortive the team was not disbanded, instead they were given a variety of recce tasks to perform in conjunction with AA3. He writes:

'During defensive operations in November 1941, First Lieutenant Wolff of Reconnaissance Battalion 3, was in a covering position behind a sandhill, and observed a tank-protected supply column in the Gambut area. He also saw that a single British car followed this column at a distance of over a kilometre. When it approached his position he barred the car's passage and laid his gun on it, thus forcing it to stop. Before he could say anything, the passengers in the car shouted to him, "Are you from Reconnaissance Battalion 3 or 33?" ("*Sind Sie von der Aufklärungsabteilung 3 oder 33?*") – and this was said in German without any trace of a foreign accent! Lt Wolff pulled over, jumped out of his reconnaissance car, and both the passengers in the other car invited him to have a glass of whisky, when he declared them as his prisoners. They were two English captains who had just returned from leave in Cairo, where

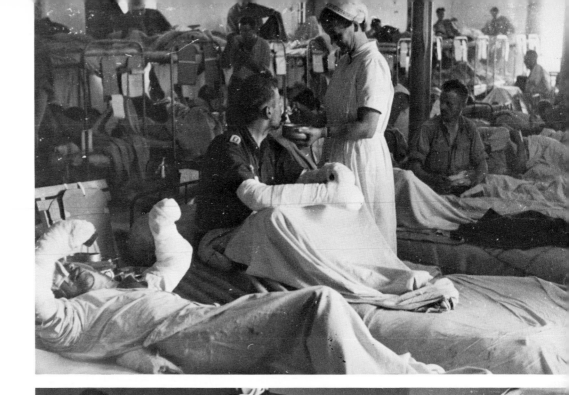

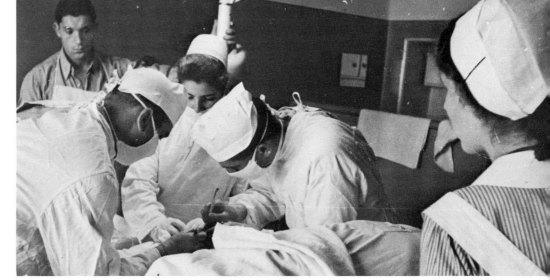

Above right: A crowded hospital ward. Here a German Red Cross nurse feeds a wounded sergeant-major (Oberfeldwebel).
/*Bundesarchiv, Koblenz*

Right: An operation in progress.
/*Bundesarchiv, Koblenz*

Below: Generalmajor Froehlich, the Luftwaffe Commander Africa, talks to a wounded airman.
/*Col T. Bock*

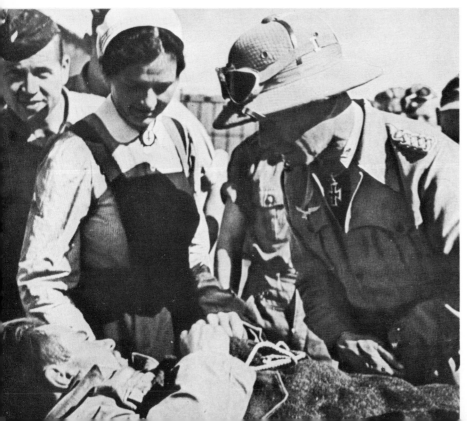

they had heard of the British offensive and now intended to return to their units as soon as possible. They had their whole leave luggage still with them.

'Major von Wechmar, then commander of Reconnaissance Battalion 3, handed these two captains over to me for delivery to a prisoner of war camp. On this day, all our connections to friendly units were cut off. At dusk, Major von Wechmar gave orders for a breakout. "I will drive ahead, and when I run into British units, I will fire off three green Verey lights and the whole Battalion will turn around. Hauptmann Kiel is in charge on the opposite side, and in case he bumps into British units, he in turn will discharge green Verey lights. Then again everyone will face about until we can find a point to break out". One of the English captains was with me in my car, and my orderly officer, Lieutenant Toni Streit, had the other one in his car.

Above: Moving wounded to a hospital ship. Loading up ambulances to take them onto the dock side.
/*Bundesarchiv, Koblenz*

Left: Walking wounded boarding a hospital ship. Hospital ships were a sore point with Rommel. He was furious when he heard that the British had been pulling them into Malta for examination. He protested, but later found to his embarrassment, that the Italians were sending petrol in the double bottoms of hospital ships. 'How can I protest against British interference with hospital ships when you do things like that?', he demanded. (*Rommel* by Desmond Young)./*IWM*

Forty more British prisoners of war were on our truck. The English captain who was driving in my car spoke perfect German. He had studied for several terms in Heidelberg. This *Orlog* (old German word for 'War') was capital fun to him, and after several green Verey lights had been fired from both sides, he croaked: "Herr Major, today you'll become *my* prisoner of war after all!"

'Finally, we were successful in breaking through the midst of a British supply column whose vehicles were driving past us in rapid succession and of which we "encouraged" three petrol trucks to join us. This caused our two captains to get very angry! There was no chance to head for a prisoner of war camp so the prisoners remained in our cars for three or four days. They shared our rations, let us partake of their inexhaustible supply of whisky, took full cover with us when we were fired upon, and even sympathised with all events in companionship. They were indeed toppers! Finally we arrived in Bardia where we handed over all our prisoners of war to the Italian garrison. This was not at all in agreement with the two captains. They had no desire whatever to get into Italian captivity. We found it hard to say goodbye to them, too'.

Above left: Stretcher cases on board a lighter being ferried out to a hospital ship. Despite the crowded conditions all look remarkably cheerful.
/*Bundesarchiv, Koblenz*

Left: A knocked out Matilda, destroyed during an attack at Sidi Omar 18 June 1941.
/*H. D. Aberger*

Above: A Bren gun carrier captured during the battle for Derna airport on 7 April 1941.
/*H. D. Aberger*

Right: A British 6 pounder anti-tank gun captured by the 4th Company 8 MG Battalion near Knightsbridge on 28 May 1942.
/*H. D. Aberger*

Epilogue

'Peace and stillness have again returned to North Africa. The rhythm of life in the few towns and villages does not disturb the quiet of the empty desert nor of the inhospitable Tunisian mountains. The roar of engines, the rattle of tank tracks, the exploding grenades and bombs, like the chattering machine guns, have fallen silent. The flotsam and jetsam of war has sunk beneath the desert sand, or has disintegrated, then been collected up and taken away as scrap. The tracks of the battalion which displayed the red eagle have vanished. Wide expanses of the desert are barred for decades by mines, which, preserved by the climate, remain a danger to man and beast. The shy gazelle have returned and along the old caravan routes, the Trighs, on which for two years the tanks and trucks rolled, the camels once again stride their leisurely way.

'Those who remain are our dead, in their graves between El Alamein and Zaghouan – and remaining too are the memories of those who survived. Memories of names which often meant little more than a heap of stones, a blocked-up well, a buried settlement or a pilgrim's grave. And linked with these names are victories and defeats, death and injury, hunger and thirst – the places at which we heaped the stones and gravel over our dead. The crosses with which we marked them have grown weather-beaten and the inscrip-

Below: Graves of dead soldiers of the 3rd, 4th Companies, the Signal troop and the Medical troop of the 1st Battalion Armoured Infantry Regiment 104 (MG 8), killed during the breakout of the 4th and 5th New Zealand Brigades on the night of 27 June 1942 at Bir Aba Batta. /H. D. Aberger

tions have faded. So, as once over the living, now over the countless graves the pitiless sun beats down, the desert wind sings its eternal song and the sandstorms cover them. Rain descends upon them and for a few hours, for a few days, the desert is transformed into a heavily scented carpet of flowers which vanish as quickly as they come. Those who lie there beneath the graves shall have no hunger or thirst, and no battle alarm shall disturb them. Only the scurrying beetles pause briefly by them. By night the myriad stars will shine down on the graves, revealing the infinity of the universe – but those who lie beneath the mounds will not see it.

'The thoughts of the survivors will always return to the North African desert. They will never be able to forget those times. And in their thoughts of those who lie at peace in the desert they will ask themselves, "Was what we did right or wrong?" And no one will give an answer and no one will make a judgement. Those who survive neither can nor wish to: the generations to come will forget the desert war, except perhaps the historians. This will become no epic war! The history of the battalion with the red eagle is a memorial, not to the war, but to its dead.

'Once again let us disturb their peace and lead them to the places whose names once rang around the world:

Tobruk – El Alamein – Tunis

In edifices resembling the old desert citadels they rest together, dumb witnesses to the meaning and paradox of war. And the words of the monument at El Alamein speak for them all:

You who stood here in battle,
Whether enemy, friend or brother,
Whether a son of Germany,
Of Italy, of England,
Valiant was your way,
Your law was the law of humanity.

Only God knows you all,
He knows your names,
And has gathered you into the ranks of the faithful.

He holds in His hands the plea
Of the living and of the dead:
The plea for peace!*

*Taken from the final chapter of *Nur Ein Bataillon* a privately circulated history of Machine Gun Battalion 8.

Below: In Memorian. Soldiers of the British Commonwealth paying their last respects at the El Alamein Memorial. All four fought against the Afrika Korps in the desert. (L to r: WO Kilmore, New Zealand; WO Anderson, Australia; RQMS Wright and Cpl Catling, England, the latter served with 4th Indian Division.)/*Associated Press*

Bibliography

Books Consulted

Bender, Roger James and Law, Richard D.: *Uniforms, Organisations and History of the Afrika Korps,* (R. James Bender Publishing)

Carell, Paul: *Die Wüstenfüsche,* (Verlag Ullstein GmbH)

Chamberlain, Peter and Ellis, Chris: *Afrika Korps 1941-42,* (Almark Publishing Co Ltd)

Davis, Brian L.: *German Army Uniforms and Insignia 1939-45,* (Arms and Armour Press)

Davies, W. J. K.: *German Army Handbook 1939-45* (Ian Allan Ltd)

Fuller, Major-General J. F. C.: *The Decisive Battles of the Western World,* (Eyre and Spottiswoode)

Fitzsimons, Bernard: (ed) *Tanks and Weapons of World War 2,* (Phoebus Publishing Co)

Hammerton, Sir John: (ed) *The Second Great War,* (Waverley Book Company Ltd and The Amalgamated Press Ltd)

Hartmann, Theodore: *Wehrmacht Divisional Signs 1938-45,* (Almark Publishing Co, Ltd)

Hart, B. H. Liddell: *The Tanks* (Cassell) and (ed) *The Rommel Papers,* (Collins; American edition Harcourt Brace Jovanovich Inc)

Hogg, Ian V.: *The Guns of World War 2,* (Macdonald & Janes Publishers Ltd)

Home, Charles Douglas: *Rommel,* (Weidenfeld & Nicolson Ltd)

Howe, George F.: *The Battle History of the 1st Armoured Division,* (Combat Forces Press)

Jackson, General W. G. E.: *The North African Campaign 1940-45,* (Batsford)

Jarrett, G. B.: *West of Alamein,* (Sentry Books)

Jewell, Derek: (ed) *Alamein and the Desert War,* (Sunday Times/Sphere Books)

Kühn, Volkmar: *Mit Rommel in der Wüste,* (Motorbuch Verlag)

Kershaw, Andrew and Close, Ian: (ed) *The Desert War,* (Phoebus Publishing Co)

Milsom, John: *German Military Transport of World War 2,* (Arms and Armour Press)

McLean, Donald B.: (ed) *Company Officer's Handbook of the German Army,* (Normount Technical Publishing)

Morris, Desmond: *The Mammals,* (Hodder & Stoughton)

Quarrie, Bruce: *Afrika Korps,* (Patrick Stephens Ltd)

Ringler, Ralph: *Endstation El Alamein,* (Ferdinand Berger & Söhne)

Spielberger, Walter J. and Feist, Uwe: *Armour in the Western Desert,* (Aero Publishing Inc)

Schmidt, Heinz Werner: *With Rommel in the Desert,* (Harrap)

Tute, Warren: *The North African War,* (Sidgwick and Jackson Ltd)

Windrow, Martin & Roffe, Michael: *The Panzer Divisions,* (Osprey)

Young, Desmond: *Rommel,* (Collins)

Young, Peter: (ed) *Atlas of the Second World War,* (Weidenfeld & Nicolson Ltd)

Balkenkrenz über Wüstensand, (Stalling)

Nur Ein Bataillon (Private)

Periodicals and Pamphlets Consulted

The Journal of the RUSI (1960 edition)

AFV Field Pocket Book 1942 (War Office)

Brief Notes on the German Army at War

Supplement No 1 – *The German Armoured Division* (1942) (War Office)

Supplement No 2 – *The Lorried Infantry Regiment* (1942) (War Office)

Supplement No 3 – *The Artillery of the Armoured Division* (1942) (War Office)

Supplement No 4 – *The German Armoured Division – Tactical Handling* (1942) (War Office)

Periodical Notes on the German Army – No 37 – *German Armoured Tactics in Libya* (1942) (War Office)

7th Armoured Division – An account of the operations in Libya – 18 Nov-27 Dec 1941 (HQ 7th Armd Div)

Die Oase – the magazine of the DAK Verband (various issues)